Pottery

Emmanuel Cooper

Macdonald Guidelines

Editorial manager
Chester Fisher
Series editor
Anne Furniss
Designer
Peter Benoist
Picture researcher
Jenny de Gex
Production
Penny Kitchenham

First published 1976
Reprinted 1979
Macdonald Educational Ltd
Holywell House, Worship Street
London EC2A 2EN

ISBN 0 356 06001 2 (paperback edition)
ISBN 0 356 06401 8 (cased edition)

Made and printed by
Waterlow (Dunstable) Limited

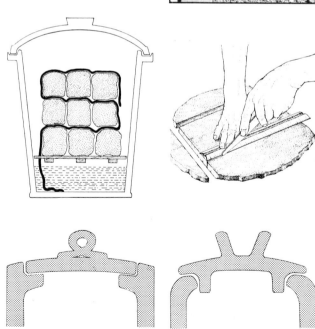

Contents

3

Introducing clay

Of all the commonly available raw materials, clay is one of the oldest and most useful. Most of us are familiar with the sticky clay which clings to boots and shoes after a walk in the country. If you are a gardener, you will be very aware of the qualities of this tough, resilient material after digging down a few feet. Our ancient ancestors were also aware of clay—they may have picked it up from the river bank or discovered its natural outcrops, and on squeezing it found it has many admirable qualities.

First of all it can be formed and shaped while it is soft without breaking. This plastic quality of clay results from the actual plate-like shape of the clay particles and their ability to surround themselves with a layer of water which enables them to slide over one another without breaking apart.

As clay dries it becomes hard and retains its shape: quite considerable strength is required to break it. Dry clay cannot resist the effects of water, which causes it to lose its shape and become soft and malleable.

Building bricks

Over the centuries, common clay has been used to make utensils and vessels for food; as well as for building large and small storage holders for grain and other produce. It was and still is used for the manufacture of bricks, a technology which has been vividly recorded in the Old Testament of the Bible.

Nine thousand years ago when nomadic hunters were beginning to settle by rivers buildings were made out of "adobes", sun-dried bricks cut out of slabs of natural clay. Later the bricks were made in

◀ Egyptians making bricks. In the bottom row the brickmakers are mixing up the clay and loading it into containers before forming it into brick shapes.

▶ Villagers carrying pots in Nigeria. Clay is used not only for making the water pots which can be seen in the foreground, but also for building the large granaries in the background. These are given thatched roofs to keep out the rain.

rectangular wooden moulds, and later still bricks were kiln fired to give them strength.

Today, the many ceramic processes include not only huge brick-making factories but industrial concerns such as those centred in Britain in Stoke-on-Trent, which make domestic pots. There are also high precision processes in which small and delicate ceramic parts are made for jet aircraft and rockets.

For potters, however, clay is still a direct, simple material which can be handled and modelled as we please. It probably holds much the same attraction for potters today as it did for our ancestors.

What is clay?

Clay is formed from igneous granitic rock which is broken down by nature through denudation and erosion. Gradually the particles become sufficiently small to be affected by physical and chemical changes and clay is formed. The process is slow and is spread over millions of years. Beds of clay occur almost everywhere a few feet below the surface, though not all are of much use to the potter.

Commercially available outcrops are relatively rare and good workable clay is a valuable commodity. Deposits of such

clay were eagerly sought by our ancestors, who would go miles to fetch the clay they required. Even today some American Indian potters travel several miles to fetch their clay.

Basically there are two sorts of clay—primary and secondary. Primary clay is deposited on the site of its parent rock; it is usually pure in composition, white in colour and is not very plastic. Examples are the china clay deposits in Cornwall in the U.K.; Alabama, Georgia and South Carolina in the U.S.A.; Meissen in Germany and Limoges in France.

The clay most of us are familiar with is secondary clay, which has been moved over many years from the site on which it was formed and deposited elsewhere. Secondary clays range in colour from red to yellow to grey to black and, in contrast to primary clays, they are usually very plastic and can be moulded and shaped easily.

Secondary clays are found almost everywhere a few feet below the surface, though not always in large amounts. Commercially such clays are sold as ball clays or marls.

Working with clay

In its soft, plastic state clay can be built up into a great variety of forms, using many different techniques. A small ball of clay can be pinched with the fingers to make a round pot which could be used for drinking or ladling.

Large shapes can be built by laying rings or coils of clay on top of each other to build up walls. Each coil is smeared or welded onto the coil below. This was the method used by potters of the beaker period, over two thousand years ago, and is still used in many parts of the world, particularly in Africa where some tribes use the technique to make water and cooking pots.

Flat slabs of clay can be used to build pots with flat walls and square corners—a technique in use in parts of the Middle East for thousands of years. The slabs are pressed, rolled or cut flat and then welded together to form a pot.

A quick method of pot building which dates far back into antiquity is with the use of a mould or former. In this technique clay is either smeared or pressed inside a hollow mould such as a coconut shell or old pot, or over a hump mould such as a stone, to form a pot.

The potter's wheel is the most sophisticated technique and the ease with which a potter transforms a clay lump into a tall pot is fascinating, but it belies the skill necessary for the work. Control such as this is only achieved after a great deal of practice.

▶ The earliest known pots were made in Catal Huyuk in Anatolia in about 6000 B.C. They usually had red geometrical decoration on a cream slip in bold design. The slip and paint were often burnished to give a slight shine.

▲ Pots made by different methods. The large garden pot is coiled; the small box with diagonal slip-trailed decoration and the flat dish are moulded and the small bowl is pinched. The square pot is made from slabs and the bottle-shaped pot was thrown on the wheel.

The first pots

It is more than likely that people used clay for other purposes long before they made pots. They used coloured clays as pigments for cave paintings and used it to build shelters. They also modelled clay to make small votive figures which were associated with fertility rites and religious beliefs; these objects were not merely decorative but served an important function. Gradually as tribes settled and the need for storage vessels increased, clay was used for making pots.

The oldest known pots come from Anatolia and consist of hand-built bowls and bottles which have powerful and bold geometrical designs painted on them after firing. These wares date from about 6000 B.C. and are finely made, suggesting that pottery making was a long established activity at this time, though so far nothing is known about earlier work.

The new techniques used by archaeologists such as carbon dating methods allow accurate estimates of age to be made, and on recent evidence dates are being pushed back further and further into the past. This is where pottery finds are so useful, for generally speaking they remain intact (unless broken) for thousands of years. Today, they are a rich source of material for the archaeologist and sociologist as well as the potter.

How a pot is made

1. Most potters buy ready-prepared clay and few carry out much clay preparation. Clay is bought in its plastic state and consists of blends of several clays together with other materials such as sand, grog or feldspar. Before the clay is used it must be wedged and kneaded to make it even and free of air bubbles.
2. One method of making a pot is to roll the clay into coils which are built up on top of each other and welded together. There are many methods of handbuilding pots and most use plastic clay.

3. Most clay takes a day or two to dry to the leatherhard stage, when work can be done to the surface of the pot. Here it is being smoothed, using a hacksaw blade pulled diagonally across the surface of the pot.
4. At this stage the pot can be decorated. On this pot a tool is being used to make an incised pattern round the neck. Other forms of decoration are reliefs and painted techniques.
5. When the pot is completely dry, which can take a week or two depending on the thickness of the clay, it is biscuit

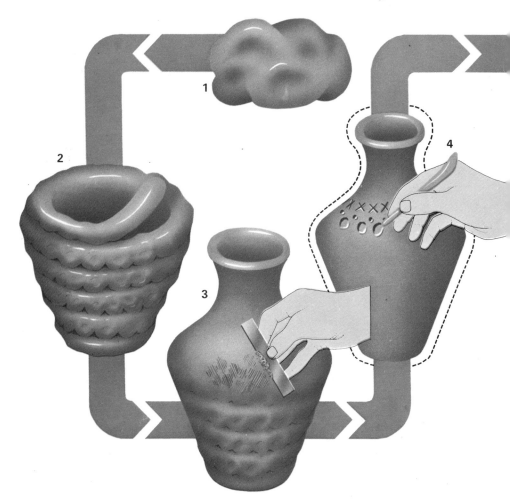

fired to render it strong and porous. All studio pottery is biscuit fired to 980°C.

6. After the biscuit firing the pot is covered with glaze. This is a liquid mixture of carefully selected materials which will melt in the kiln to form a glassy surface on the pot. Glaze is applied here by dipping; other processes include pouring, painting and spraying. Glazes can be matt or shiny, smooth or rough, clear or coloured.

7. The pot is fired a second time in the glaze or glost firing. This is to a higher temperature than the biscuit firing and, as well as melting the glaze, reduces the porosity of the body and makes it stronger. From the making stage to the glaze fired pot, shrinkage is about 8%. Earthenware glaze temperature is 1040°–1150°C., stoneware 1200°–1260°C.

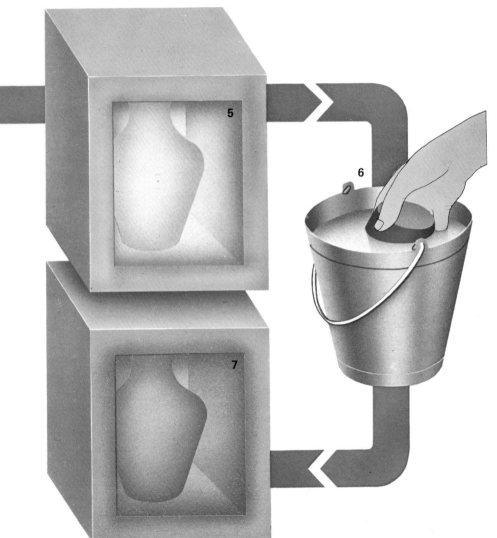

The development of form

Shape and form depend very much on the method of making and the material that is being used. A pot which is pinched in the hand will be rounded, fairly small and probably have uneven walls. Coil pots grow slowly and the shape can be given a sharp change in direction; usually these shapes are rounded. The invention of the wheel and its development as a machine on which pots could be quickly thrown brought many changes to pottery, both to the techniques involved and to the end-product.

The invention and development of the wheel occurred over a long period of time. Building pots by hand and turning them round on a stone or broken piece of pot was a wheel of sorts, but it was not until the wheelhead was fixed onto a spindle that the first potter's wheel was used. This slow, or hand, wheel as it is called was turned slowly by the potter, or pushed by an assistant. Wheels such as these came into use in the Middle East some 5,000 years ago and very much affected the nature of the pottery processes.

Before throwing on the wheel clays must be carefully cleaned of small stones, and some clays are not suitable for thrown work. The wheel also affected shape, for it is a process which makes all pots round and symmetrical. Angles of pots are also changed; sharp, carinated forms are difficult to throw, whilst smooth flowing curves occur easily.

The use of the wheel also altered the organisation of pottery-making processes. The higher level of technology and specialist skills needed to make pots turned pot-making more into an industry situated according to favourable working conditions and markets.

Different wheels were developed in different parts of the world. In Italy a crank was fitted to the wheel spindle, in France the fly-wheel was made heavy and was kicked round.

Japan

In Japan, a stick was used to give the wheel momentum, softer clay was used and often the shapes were slightly uneven. As pots were an integral part of the Japanese Tea Ceremony and associated with Zen Buddhism, which admired the "natural" qualities of materials and pro-

▲ Sitting cross-legged on the ground in front of a traditional Indian potter's wheel, the potter will produce quantities of small cups very much as his ancestors have done for hundreds of years.

enabled the crisp Greek forms to be made. These tended to conform to established designs for particular uses. Complex shapes were thrown in section which were joined together at the leatherhard stage, and the final shape was achieved by putting the pot back on the wheel and turning the surface with a sharp tool.

Decoration was carried out by painters who specialised in this work, and on the best pieces they signed their names alongside that of the potter. The red and black designs were obtained by the use of a specially prepared slip of fine red clay. The final success of the painter and potter was achieved in the kiln, when careful control of the one firing process was essential.

▲ A Greek Attic black-figured amphora, showing Achilles slaying Penthesilea, the queen of the Amazons. 540–530 B.C.

cesses, this did not matter. Hence what may look casual or roughly made to the untutored Western eye, looks rich, sensuous and beautiful to the eyes of a Japanese.

Ancient Greece

Greek pots are some of the finest examples of thrown wares that exist from the ancient world. In ancient Greece, potters worked in small workshops to produce a wide range of domestic ware as well as the famous black and red wares.

Excellent deposits of yellow or red coloured clays outside Corinth and Athens, the two major centres, ensured a good supply of strong throwing clay which

▲ This illustration comes from a 16th-century book on the arts and techniques of pottery, written and drawn by the Italian potter Cipriano Piccolpasso. It shows a potter at work on his wheel trimming a pot at the leatherhard stage.

Kilns and firing

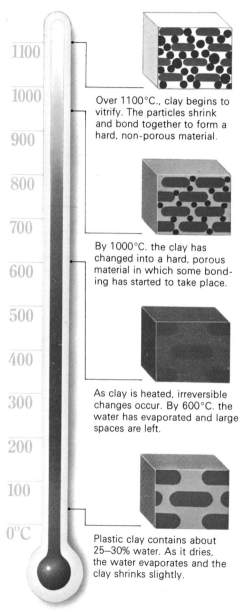

Over 1100°C., clay begins to vitrify. The particles shrink and bond together to form a hard, non-porous material.

By 1000°C. the clay has changed into a hard, porous material in which some bonding has started to take place.

As clay is heated, irreversible changes occur. By 600°C. the water has evaporated and large spaces are left.

Plastic clay contains about 25–30% water. As it dries, the water evaporates and the clay shrinks slightly.

Fire was one of the world's most important discoveries. From it, came the discovery of the effect of heat on clay that enabled vessels to be made which are not affected by water. Perhaps it was discovered by smearing clay on the inside of a bird's nest which was then used to transport hot cinders. This would leave behind a primitive form of fired clay. Or possibly clay was used to line a hole in the ground in which fire was kept and again a primitive fired vessel was formed. It is estimated that the earliest discoveries with regard to the effects of heat and clay were made some ten to twelve thousand years ago.

Irreversible changes

When clay is heated it undergoes several changes which, after a certain point become irreversible. Clay heated to 100°C will become physically completely dry, yet it can be soaked down in water and reused. If heating is continued until around 600°–700°C., when it just begins to show a very dull red colour, irreversible changes have occurred in the chemical structure of the clay. At this stage the material is soft, crumbly and porous, but it will not disintegrate in water nor will it be plastic.

If heat is increased until 900°–1000°C further changes occur. The clay particles begin to bond together and become stronger. Any carboneous material, such as the organic remains of plants, will burn away, leaving a material which is bright and clean and may be quite unlike the original colour. For example, ordinary flower pots made out of red clay will now appear a bright terracotta colour and are strong and porous. Many black clays fire

Nigerian bonfire firing

▲ Pots, made from local clay, must be completely dry before they can be fired. If not, the rapid rise in heat will cause them to crack. Occasionally dry grass is burned inside them beforehand to ensure they are dry. The pots are stacked on dry wood, and arranged so that as the wood burns they do not fall and break. Dry grass is put over the stacked pots and set alight.

▶ The firing is over very quickly, and the pots are hooked out from the ashes while they are still hot.

13

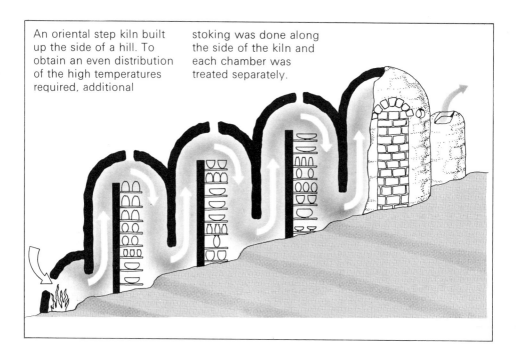

An oriental step kiln built up the side of a hill. To obtain an even distribution of the high temperatures required, additional stoking was done along the side of the kiln and each chamber was treated separately.

an ivory buff colour because the carboneous matter formed from rotted organic material has burnt away.

Most primitive firing in traditional potteries in such places as Nigeria are taken to a temperature of around 800°C. Many local red firing clays are rendered hard and vitrified at this temperature.

The first kilns

The first kilns were built in the Middle East. A fire box was constructed under an open grid of clay supports and on these, pots were packed. They were covered over with a layer of old fired pots or turfs with a chimney hole in the top and a stacking chamber was formed. Retained heat in the chamber made it possible to achieve higher temperatures than with an open firing. This was the first updraught kiln.

Gradually kilns became more permanent structures and the pots were protected from the flames, with the result that decoration and glaze could be used which would not be marked by the flame. Greater control of the firings also enabled the temperature in the kiln to be monitored. Typical Roman kilns were circular in plan with a platform perforated with holes raised on a central post. The fuel was burned in the chamber beneath the platform and the pots arranged on it; wood for firing the kiln was fed through a straight passage which helped control the inflow of air. Kilns such as these have continued in use in the Middle East and in the West for hundreds of years.

The Far East

Potters in China built different sorts of kilns. Instead of constructing them above ground they built them in the side of hills. The fire was made at the bottom so that the chamber in which the pots were stood became more a part of the chimney. A damper arrangement at the top of the kiln helped to control the outlet of hot gases and the kiln built up heat and retained it. The advantage of the hill kiln was its ability to achieve high temperatures. Because the heat loss was controlled by the damper and the earth insulation, temperatures of around 1200°C were obtained, particularly near the fire box. At this temperature most clays become hard and vitrified and in fact become stoneware.

As these kilns became more sophisticated they were built in a series of steps partly below ground, partly above ground, and some were divided into different chambers. Small stoking holes were built in the sides of the kiln so that even temperatures could be obtained.

These kilns became widespread in the Far East, though they varied in detail from place to place. Until comparatively recently, they were far more efficient and capable of achieving much higher temperatures than any kilns in the West. As late as the 17th century, brick-built one-chamber kilns were used in Europe, which had a probable maximum temperature of 1000°C.

The Industrial Revolution

The Industrial Revolution brought great advances in kiln design and construction and by the beginning of the 19th century kilns were in use in European factories which equalled those in China.

The first successful attempts to manufacture porcelain in Europe in the 18th century were partly made possible by the development of a kiln which would reach 1300°C. In Europe, bricks made out of refractory clay were used for the elongated bottle shape kiln, and the fire box was carefully constructed with cast iron grate bars. This increased the fuel burning efficiency of the coal and coke retained heat.

Updraught bottle kilns were in use for pottery production until replaced over the last 50 years by modern electric, gas and oil kilns. Bottle kilns are round in shape with several fire mouths at the bottom. The flames travel upwards around the wares and out through the chimney at the top. The pots are protected from the flame by being packed in ceramic boxes, called saggars (an abbreviation of "safeguard").

The European downdraught kiln was the other major type. It was round or rectangular in shape with fire mouths at the sides and flue outlets in the floor. With this arrangement high and even temperatures can be achieved.

Today most kilns are fired by oil, gas or electricity and the hard work and smoke of the potteries has gone for ever.

▲ Bottle kilns used to be a familiar part of the industrial landscape in the pottery town of Stoke-on-Trent, England. Fired by coal and coke, they created a highly polluted, smokey atmosphere. Now, most of these kilns have been replaced by modern tunnel kilns fired by electricity.

Colourful earthenware

Earthenware is the general name used to describe low-fired pottery; it is usually made out of terracotta or cream-coloured clay and is slightly porous. Some earthenware pots were finished by burnishing, that is rubbing with a smooth stone, while others were covered in glaze.

Some of the finest earthenware pots were made in Egypt. The fine Nile muds rendered a smooth, red firing clay which could be worked with great refinement. In the Badarian culture flat bowls and dishes were built by hand, which are still admired from a technical and aesthetic point of view.

Tall pots with pointed bases which could stand upright in soft, sandy soils and safely store wine and oil were also

▲ This earthenware urn has a spiral design in red and black. It was hand-built in China between 2000 and 1500 B.C.

made. The surfaces of the pots were polished or burnished by rubbing when leatherhard with a smooth tool made out of stone or bone. This had the effect of giving not only a rich lustrous surface but one which added physical strength to the pot. These jars are also notable for their black rims, obtained by firing the pots upside down in wood ashes to prevent the flame from reaching the rim.

The first glazes

Pottery fired to earthenware temperatures is porous and liquids seep through. The technique of covering the clay surface with a layer of glass to make it waterproof was first used in the Middle East some five thousand years ago. The first glazed objects, known as Egyptian paste, were made out of a special mixture of sand, soda and copper oxide which, when mixed with water, was moulded and modelled into such things as beads and amulets. As the objects dried the soluble salts in the mixture migrated to the surface, and in the firing formed a semi-shiny rich green glaze which ranged in colour from pale blue to bright turquoise. Later, other colours were also discovered, amongst them violet, apple green and yellow. Delicate small bottles were also made in Egyptian paste.

The Assyrians and Babylonians were the first to discover how to use glaze on the surface of fired clay—first on bricks used to ornament palace walls, and later on actual pots. The glaze was often a pleasant turquoise blue colour, though the technical problems involved in achieving a strong glaze took many years to overcome.

Roman potters learned from the Egyptians the art of glazing and produced green

covered wares at pottery centres throughout the Empire, notably in Gaul (France) and Germania (Germany). Instead of soda or potash salts, lead was used in the glaze which gave a stronger and more easily applied mixture. Lead glaze continued to be used in Europe until modern times, particularly by country potters for local products.

Some earthenware glazes were coloured and used over white slips. Typical is the rich turquoise blue glaze on the Syrian vase. Other potters used clear transparent lead glazes directly over decoration.

Slip decoration

In Britain the glaze was used over designs made by using coloured clays called slips. They were painted, poured or trailed (like icing sugar) onto the leatherhard clay. In certain places such as Wrotham, Kent, or in the Midland, Staffordshire area, very

▲ A Syrian vase, thrown out of white earthenware clay with black painted Arabic script under a richly coloured turquoise glaze. Late 12th century.

▶ A selection of the tin-glazed earthenware known as Delftware. The Majolica pot (right) was made in the Netherlands in 1550. The English plate and Dutch drug jar were made in the 17th century.

▲ This Thomas Toft dish, made out of red earthenware and decorated with red, black and cream slip, shows a mermaid. It is lead glazed and was made in Staffordshire, England, between 1650 and 1700.

century onwards, tin glaze was used in Spain to make the beautiful and ornate Hispano-Moresque wares. From Spain the technique travelled to Italy where it was known as Maiolica or Majolica. In time Italian potters took it to France, Holland and eventually England. Here they were known as Delft wares, and were richly painted and colourfully decorated.

distinctive styles developed which were obviously carried out by skilled decorators.

These pots were usually made for ordinary domestic use, in the home or on the farm, and were produced very much for a local market. The Toft family were great decorators and they must have spent a considerable time working on their large splendid dishes, usually made to commemorate or celebrate special occasions.

Tin glaze

White porcelain imported into the Middle East in the ninth and tenth centuries was greatly admired and potters sought to imitate it. They discovered that ashes of tin (tin oxide) added to the transparent glaze made it white and opaque. As well as imitating the whiteness of porcelain, this gave a good surface for painted designs. The use of glazes opacified by tin spread into and across Europe. From the 13th

▲ An Albarello, earthenware with white tin-glaze and painted in-glaze decoration. These pots were used to hold medicines and their concave sides allowed them to be grasped easily. Made in Italy in the 15th century.

Stoneware and saltglaze

Stoneware describes pots fired to a temperature over 1200°C when clay becomes hard, vitrified and impervious—very similar, in fact, to stone. To make stoneware, suitable refractory clay must be available as well as kilns capable of achieving these high temperatures. Both were known in China over two thousand years ago.

Glazes for use at stoneware temperature were slower to be developed, mainly because stoneware vessels are impervious, so for practical purposes glaze is not necessary. Chinese potters using hill kilns found that when fuel burned with a slightly smokey flame this turned the pots a rich brown colour.

Glaze effects obtained in special sorts of kiln firings were much admired in China. One story by Tang Y'ing, which illustrates how prized such effects were, tells of the divine potter T'ung. T'ung produced a blood red coloured glaze which was greatly admired by the Emperor who wanted it repeated. The potter continually failed to achieve the glaze again. In complete desperation, he threw himself on the fire. When his assistants unpacked the kiln they found all the pots covered with the highly prized red glaze.

Ash glazes

Potters also noticed that wood ash carried inside the kiln from the fire mouth settled on the shoulders of pots and inside bowls where it melted and combined with the clay surface to form a mottled glaze. Also discovered was the fact that some granitic and feldspathic rocks, when ground to a fine powder and dusted onto the clay surface, also melted to form milky white glazes. Gradually, over the years, the Chinese potters perfected their glazes and stoneware pots.

Combinations of wood ash and feldspar or wood ash and clay were used to produce semi matt, silky textured glazes that have become synonymous with Chinese pottery. The glazes were often coloured dark olive green and these were given the name celadon, meaning green glaze. Most of these glaze effects depended on a reducing atmosphere in the kiln (when insufficient oxygen is present), and can only be obtained under these conditions.

Chinese glazes

The ideal glaze of the Chinese stoneware potter was one which was dense, smooth and semi-translucent in appearance. Unlike earthenware glazes which remain as a layer on the surface of the clay, stoneware glazes fuse much more with the clay body and the two layers are not so separate. For this reason and because of the higher temperatures involved, stoneware glazes are more subdued in colour. Old Chinese writers refer to such glazes as "fat and unctuous" like "mutton fat" or "congealed lard": evocative descriptions.

◀ A Chinese stoneware bottle of the T'ang dynasty (618–906 A.D.). The body and neck were thrown in two separate parts and joined together at the leatherhard stage. It has a creamy white glaze.

▶ A Japanese thrown pot with glaze on the shoulder caused by wood ash settling on the pot during the high temperature firing. The Japanese were very fond of these "natural" effects. It is thought that these were the first stoneware glazes to be developed.

As Chinese potters developed potting techniques, they aimed more and more for a whiter stoneware body, on which the glazes would be whiter and brighter. At times this led to glaze effects in which a fine network of cracks appeared in the glaze, due to unequal shrinkage between the body and the glaze. The Chinese call this crackle glaze and deliberately sought it as a decorative effect.

Like white wares, the production of red glazes were continually being sought by Chinese potters. Glazes with crimson or purple blotches were obtained by firing glazes containing copper in a heavy reducing atmosphere. Today such glazes are admired but the old Chinese connoisseurs spoke of them with contempt as like "pig's liver", "horse's dung" or "nose mucus". Later on other red and crimson glazes were discovered known as "precious-stone red" because it was alleged that crushed rubies were used in their preparation.

Saltglaze stoneware

Europe's greatest single contribution to ceramic technology apart from the discovery of hard paste porcelain was the discovery of saltglazed stoneware by German potters in the 14th century. The clay available in the German Rhineland is rich in silica which makes it able to withstand high temperatures. Saltglaze is produced by throwing common salt into the kiln at top temperature 1200°–1250°C. The salt vaporizes and combines with the clay body to produce a thin, glassy film on the surface of the pot.

The colour and texture of the glaze varies according to the iron content of the body and any application of vitrifiable iron-bearing clay. The surface is often mottled and coloured cream or brown, depending on the clay used. The rich clay deposits in the Rhineland made it the most important centre of stoneware manufacture. The Rhine also served as a convenient means of transport and large quantities of pots were sold not only on the German market but also exported to other European countries.

Saltglaze has the great advantage of being both strong and resistant to acid attack. Consequently it was useful for all types of storage vessels and any applied decoration was picked out and heightened by the glaze. This encouraged stamped decorative reliefs to be applied to the surface of the pot. Designs were obtained from seals, coils, medals and ornamental plaques, as well as some freely modelled reliefs.

Domestic pottery

A wide range of domestic pots was produced, many to be used as drinking-mugs, tankards, wine and ale bottles. Cardinal Bellarmine, a medieval priest who condemned the drinking of alcohol, had his bearded face stamped on the side of the wine bottles. From this such bottles came to be known as Bellarmines, no doubt as a mark of disrespect to the unpopular priest.

Today saltglaze is almost exclusively made by studio potters as the pollution which arises from the kiln when salt is added makes it dangerous and unpopular, in this environmentally-conscious age. It is relatively harmless in small quantities and under carefully regulated conditions, but these are not usually available except in country districts or in art schools. Even then, great care must be taken to avoid breathing in the poisonous fumes. This firing should never take place in an enclosed area where the possibility of breathing in fumes is greatest.

▲ A German saltglaze stoneware Bellarmine. The applied relief decoration showing a bearded face is supposed to represent Cardinal Bellarmine, notorious for forbidding the drinking of alcohol. The Crucifixion is shown with German austerity and the Apostles are depicted in the frieze. Made about 1575.

◄ This detail from a painting by Pieter Bruegel shows Rhenish saltglazed stoneware drinking vessels. The typical mottlings of the saltglaze can be seen. It was painted in about 1567, when the saltglaze industry was well-established.

Priceless porcelain

Porcelain is a white, translucent type of stoneware made from a special clay body which consists of china clay (kaolin) and petuntse (a Chinese rock similar to Cornish stone). Like jade, porcelain was highly esteemed and treasured by the Chinese. Literature exhorting its virtue, sometimes in vivid and extravagant language, grew up around it.

Porcelain pots were known outside China by the tenth century and were highly valued, partly for their rarity and also because of the beauty of the material. Its method of manufacture was to remain a closely-kept Chinese secret until it was re-discovered in Germany at the beginning of the 18th century.

Some of the earliest Chinese porcelain was made during the T'ang dynasty when potters produced for the first time a translucent white body. Soleyman, an Arab traveller, wrote in 851 A.D. of the fine white clay in China from which they made vases with the "transparency of glass bottles".

Potters in the Sung dynasty further mastered the art of producing porcelain: one of the aims was to produce porcelain which resembled green jade in strength and permanence and this was achieved. Delicate white and pale blue wares were also produced, some lightly incised with lotus petals, chrysanthemums and bird-designs.

In 1260, Kublai Khan came to power in China and opened up highways for travel and trade. During this time Marco Polo went to China and brought back to Europe stories of the amazing things he saw and examples of the skills of Chinese potters.

Ming

During the later Ming dynasty the art of the potter flourished yet again. The secret of underglaze painting in cobalt blue had been learnt from the Middle East and under patronage from the Ming Emperors, the Imperial factory was built at Ching-tê-Chên.

The white porcelain now served as a background for painted designs of increasing brilliance. Bright painted enamel

▲ A Chinese blue and white porcelain bottle, made during the Ming dynasty. It has cobalt blue underglaze decoration showing the Imperial dragon. The dragon was the symbol used for the Emperor. Most Chinese designs carried powerful symbolic meaning. The design has run slightly under the glaze.

◄ Making porcelain in 18th-century China was a highly skilled process in which only the purest of materials could be used. In this picture the pots are being packed in saggars which are then stacked inside the kiln.

decoration was needed which had to be fixed in a low temperature fixing. Designs painted in cobalt blue underglaze were perfected and the famous blue and white wares were produced. Generally, Chinese porcelain became more decorative and colourful and maximum refinements of technique were achieved which have never been equalled.

The secret discovered

Porcelain seen outside China stimulated potters to attempt to discover the secret of its manufacture. However, without the essential raw materials and the necessary knowledge of high temperature kiln firing, they were unsuccessful and turned instead to imitating its whiteness.

One of the first, though shortlived, successful attempts to make a translucent body was made in Florence, in 1575. This was the so-called Medici porcelain, produced for the Medici family. It was made from clay mixed with a glass frit, and was difficult to work. When fired, it was really quite unlike true porcelain.

The first real European hard paste porcelain (meaning fired to a high temperature) was made in Germany by Johann Böttger, and as a result of his discovery the royal factory was set up at Meissen under his direction in 1710. Though the secret was closely guarded and told only to a few potters, workmen were bribed to disclose the process involved, and in due course a rival factory was set up at Vienna.

This was followed by many others and it became fashionable for the nobility to set up their own porcelain factories. In due

course the Archbishop-Elector of Mainz patronized one at Höchst and Frederick the Great at Berlin, though Meissen remained the technical and aesthetic superior. As well as producing fine tablewares with superb decoration many beautiful figures were modelled for this factory by Johann Joachim Kaendler.

Royal patronage

Soon the secret of high temperature porcelain manufacture had spread throughout Europe, though many factories produced soft paste porcelain, which has a special frit added to the body, and is fired to a lower temperature. Of the French factories, the royal works at Sèvres eclipsed all the others. In 1753 the factory was given the title of "Royal Manufacture" and at various times hard and soft paste porcelain was produced.

In England no such royal patronage existed, and the production of porcelain

---

Johann Friedrich Böttger (1682–1719) was a German chemist who was employed by Augustus the Strong, Elector of Saxony, to discover the secret of making gold. Though unsuccessful in this field he discovered, during the process of his experiments, the secrets of true Chinese porcelain. The Elector was delighted and imprisoned Böttger lest he should reveal his secret. A factory was set up at Meissen under Böttger's direction for the production of porcelain for the first time in Europe. But it was not long before the secret leaked out and spread all over Europe.

was left to well-to-do individuals; factories producing soft paste porcelain were set up for example at Chelsea, Derby and Lowestoft.

A particular English development was the invention of bone china by Josiah Spode towards the end of the 18th century, made by adding calcined animal bones to the clay. Few factories made true, or hard paste, porcelain with the notable exception of the Worcester Porcelain Company, which is still in operation. At this factory, domestic work and modelled figures and animals are made. These are all fired to a temperature of over 1300°C.

Many studio potters make hard paste porcelain and due to the discovery of more plastic clays, the new bodies have excellent making and fired properties which have attracted much interest.

▼ The factory at Sèvres on the outskirts of Paris eclipsed all other French factories. In this workshop, potters are at work finishing pots on the wheel and modelling figures.

▲ Meissen porcelain figure of the potter at work on the continental type of kick wheel, which is turned by pushing the fly wheel with the foot. Meissen was the leading German porcelain factory.

The art of decoration

As soon as pots could be protected in the kiln from being marked by the flame, they began to be decorated before being fired. In the Middle East, painted decoration using coloured clay pigments dated back to 3000 B.C.; patterns consisted of geometrical motifs as well as stylised representations of the human figure and animals. This decorative element in Middle Eastern ceramics continued to play an important role and was picked up and further developed by the Islamic potters on glazed wares.

The use of glaze enabled many different sorts of decoration to be used. Underglaze is painted on to the pot and the glaze goes over it (i.e. underglaze blue); in-glaze is painted on top of the unfired glaze (i.e. tin glazed ware); on-glaze or enamel decoration is applied on top of the fired glaze, and fixed in a low temperature firing.

The art of Islam

All these techniques were used at different times by the Islamic potters whose religion forbids the depicting of human and animal life. Instead, the potters concentrated on semi-abstract flower and leaf designs, on geometrical and intricate patterns and on the use of flowing Arabic script patterns, both as designs and as inscriptions of a holy nature. White firing clays and the use of tin oxide in the glaze provided suitable surface backgrounds for decoration. Sometimes this was painted with flowing colours and sometimes it was scratched through a slip of contrasting colour.

▼ A 13th-century Persian bowl, thrown in white earthenware. It has painted decoration showing natural plants and fish forms.

▲ This Hispano-Moresque bowl with painted brown-gold lustre and underglazed blue decoration was made at Manises in Valencia, Spain, about 1420. A Portuguese ship and four dolphins as well as Arabic script form the design.

Occasionally, the religious rules were broken and animals were shown.

The Islamic religion also forbade the use of precious metals for eating from. Around the tenth century in Egypt and the Middle East, lustrous surfaces were produced on the surface of tin-glazed bowls to imitate the surface of precious metals. The technique for achieving lustre is a specialist one and few potters knew the secret. Metal oxides mixed with earth were painted on the fired glaze surface and fired a third time in a smokey kiln atmosphere. During this firing the metal is deposited on the glaze surface and if successful is later burnished to a brilliant effect.

Spanish lustreware

Lustre was produced on pots in combination with underglaze decoration, and this technique was brought to an unequalled brilliance in Spain in the 14th and 15th centuries. Decoration in different coloured lustres was combined with blue underglaze in arabesque patterns which took some elements from the Islamic culture and some from the Christian culture.

Enamel colours were also used with great success. These low temperature colours were painted on the fired glaze and refired. In Persia the painters of illuminated manuscripts were often employed to carry out the designs on flat bowls and dishes. These works are interesting, not only for the mastery of technique, but also because of the nature of the scenes depicted and the information they convey of contemporary life.

The ceramics industry

The ceramics industry is a complex, highly organized and efficient concern. Most of the processes are carried out by machine, though much skilled labour is still employed. This chart shows all the basic processes.

Mixing clay body

Making processes

Decorating and firing

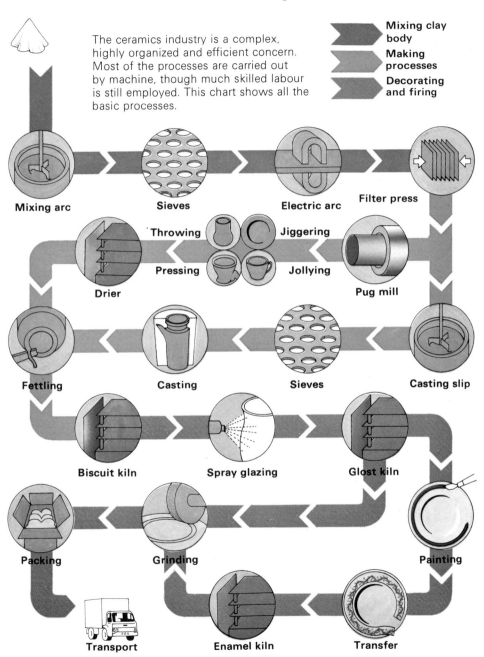

Mixing arc

Sieves

Electric arc

Filter press

Throwing

Jiggering

Pressing

Jollying

Drier

Pug mill

Fettling

Casting

Sieves

Casting slip

Biscuit kiln

Spray glazing

Glost kiln

Packing

Grinding

Painting

Transport

Enamel kiln

Transfer

Josiah Wedgwood was born in 1730. At the age of 14 he was a potter's apprentice and 15 years later set up his own business. Known as the father of modern industrial pottery, he was one of the main organisers of the industry we know today.

▲ Much modern Wedgwood ware is based on the traditional patterns, though a team of designers is constantly evolving new techniques and shapes.

▲ A range of modern industrial pottery from the Royal Copenhagen Porcelain Manufactory. The simple design and clean shapes are typical of the Scandinavian influence on modern pottery.

The Industrial Revolution

In 1750 potters were still working as small family businesses, producing ware for local markets. The advent of the Industrial Revolution changed the whole system of pottery manufacture within 50 years. Well organised factories were set up which produced finely made earthenware which was sold throughout Britain and was exported to the continent and the U.S.A. Specialised production processes, the use of carefully prepared raw materials, marketing and distribution methods were developed. Much of the credit for all this goes to Josiah Wedgwood.

Wedgwood sought to produce a cream coloured earthenware with thinly made walls, using all known technical improvements; in his work he tried to achieve greater refinements of shape and ornament. His enthusiasm for classical architecture led him to develop a neo-classical style which proved both popular and beautiful. Under his direction, a white tableware known as Queen's ware was produced as well as refined coloured body wares such as Green Jasper or Black Basalt, both of which had delicate relief modelled decoration applied on the surface.

Wedgwood helped to organise an industry which changed from being based in simple country potteries to become a highly specialised but still craft-based activity, the products of which were recognisably excellent.

Modern industrial earthenware is made from a mixture of china clay, china stone, ball clay and flint. The materials are cleaned, prepared and blended to form a suitable body. The first semi-automatic pottery-making process was tried in the mid-19th century, and today the making processes are done almost entirely by machine.

Pottery today

Reaction against growing industrialisation came from artists in the 19th century who felt that the introduction of the machine had not necessarily provided a better standard of living or well-designed objects. They saw the traditional skills of the printer, weaver, carpenter and potter disappearing in the face of growing mass production methods.

One of the leaders of the movement against the dehumanisation of factory work was William Morris. Together with his followers, he set up a workshop where skilled artisans produced goods for use in the home at what they hoped would be competitive prices.

The Arts and Crafts Movement embodied all Morris's ideas with regard to methods of production and hand skills. In 1888 the Arts and Crafts Exhibition Society was formed to display the work of artist craftsmen who sought to use traditional skills for making fairly ordinary objects. In many ways their ideas were unworkable, for hand work is an expensive method of production; nevertheless, their ideas and work had a lasting influence on much 20th-century design and thought.

Small workshops embodying the ideas of the Arts and Crafts Movement were set up in many countries. In Holland, Dutch craftsmen were influenced by Japanese Batik and German saltglazed stonewares.

In other countries, artists were at work using traditional skills and materials to produce a new art form. By 1850, French

▲ The four Martin brothers worked very much in the Arts and Crafts tradition. In their studio in Southall, Middlesex, they produced saltglazed stoneware.

▲ Bernard Leach at work in his pottery. Leach learned pottery in Japan and his work has influenced potters all over the world for the last 50 years.

studio potters were making pots which were exhibited alongside the work of painters and sculptors. Imported Chinese and Japanese stoneware shown in Europe and America for the first time proved a remarkable stimulus as potters on the continent, in the U.S.A. and in Britain tried to emulate the shapes and rich stoneware glazes.

Modern influences

Many contemporary studio potters are stimulated by the ideas and work of Bernard Leach. He set up his workshop in St Ives in 1920 after learning to be a potter in Japan.

Influences, however, are now much more diverse than from the Orient. The lively work of pop artists in the U.S.A. has affected the work of ceramists and a new branch of ceramic sculpture has arisen. These artists are concerned with using clay as a medium of expression rather than to make useful pots and results have ranged from the super-realism of miniature settees and fruit machines to the ragged casualness of the giant mixed-media sculptures.

Notable also is the growth of ceramics students, whether full-time at art school or part-time at evening class. For the student who wants to set up a home workshop, the financial outlay need not be large and in the Reference Section addresses of manufacturers and suppliers provide all the necessary information.

▼ A ceramic sculpture illustrating how the exercising of power under the cloak of consideration can lead to loss of freedom. This powerful work by Britt-Ingrid Persson, the Swedish ceramist, is typical of the concern of many modern artists.

▶ "Flowering torso" by Johnny Rolf, made from slab and handbuilt stoneware with a green, mauve and turquoise copper glaze. This imaginative modelled piece is by one of Holland's leading modern potters.

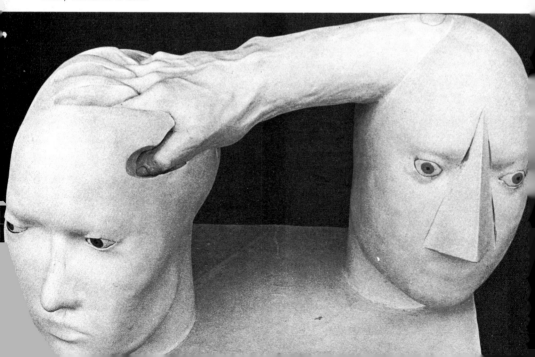

Clay and its care

Clay can be bought in small quantities from local craft shops or ordered in larger amounts from the addresses listed in the reference section. Most suppliers offer two basic clays in a plastic ready-to-use condition—a red earthenware known as terracotta and a grey stoneware. Choose the one which corresponds to your firing temperature—maximum earthenware temperature is about 1150°C and stoneware 1260°C.

Tools

Almost any tool is useful to the enterprising potter. However, a strong table with an even, smooth surface (wood is nicest) is essential. Bowls of water, a synthetic sponge for cleaning tables, a sharp knife (one from the kitchen is ideal) and small batts to stand the pot on while working are also necessary. Lollipop sticks make efficient modelling tools. Supplies catalogues list all the available speciality tools.

Wire cutter

Two sorts are required. A thick strong nylon one made from fishing line for slicing blocks of clay, and a thinner one made from twisted wire for cutting pots from the wheel.

Materials for clay care

Keeping clay in good working state involves softening it down when it is too hard and drying it out when too wet. A plaster of Paris block is useful for drying clay out.

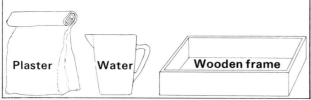

Plaster   Water   Wooden frame

Storing

Keeping clays in a good workable state saves a lot of time and energy. Sheets of polythene or polythene bags reduce evaporation to a minimum and so prevent the clay drying out. Ideally clay should be wrapped in sheets of polythene and stored in a cool, damp place. Blocks knocked square will stand closer together and retain more moisture.

Body additions

Clay is generally supplied "neat", that is without any special additions. However, for hand-building techniques (not throwing), it is often helpful to add certain other materials to the clay.

Sand, for example, can be added to open the body, leaving it less dense and more workable. Builder's sand or silver sand have their own qualities and amounts from 5—15 per cent can be added.

Grog is made from clay which has been fired and is crushed to a coarse dust. This is added to the body to reduce shrinkage, to speed up drying and make it more even. It also gives the body "tooth" and makes it pleasant to handle, giving it texture. Like sand, amounts from 5–15 per cent can be used, though not more than 15 per cent of sand and grog together should be added. To add the sand and grog, mix them with a little water and wedge them into the plastic clay.

Depending on the amount of clay drying out, it should be ready for use in a day or two.

Clay which has not dried out completely but is too hard for use can be softened by cutting the clay into lumps and wrapping them in a cloth in a bin as illustrated. Water stood at the bottom of the bin will be drawn up by the cloth and the clay will be workable in a few days.

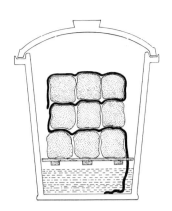

Clay care
Keeping clay in a good working condition is much easier than bringing it to the workable state. However, clay which has not been fired can be re-used, unless contaminated with plaster.

Never pour clay slops down the sink as they can settle in the drains to form a solid blockage.

Clay which has dried out completely, either as scraps or unwanted pots, can be broken up into small pieces or put into water to soften. After a day or two remove the clear water and put the wet lumpy clay, known as slurry, on a cloth on a plaster of Paris block, as illustrated. Other cloths wrapped over the clay will help it to dry out evenly.

Making a drying block
Plaster of Paris can be bought from local building suppliers or, more expensively, from a chemist as

"dental plaster". For a drying block the cheaper builder's plaster is quite satisfactory.

Again, a word of warning: do not pour any plaster down the sink, as it, too, blocks up drains.

Estimate the amount of plaster and water you will need for your block. One kilo of plaster in one litre of water will give you approximately a 1,300 cu. cm. block. Measure your ingredients and slowly sprinkle the powder into the water. Leave for two or three minutes, before gently stirring. Just as it is stiffening, pour the plaster into a flat cardboard box to set.

When the plaster has set, the cardboard can be removed and the plaster surface smoothed with a metal rule. The block will need to dry before it can be used.

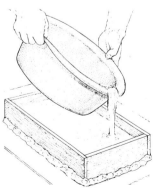

35

Preparing the clay

Greater strength can be obtained if the particles are moving in similar directions.

Clay preparation, therefore, is an essential part of the pottery process, for it not only ensures an even mixture but makes it more strong and workable.

Clay preparation

Clay is made up of flat plate-like particles which, when separated by a layer of water, slide over each other; this is what gives clay its plastic or malleable quality.

A good workable clay in a plastic state contains about 25–30 per cent water which is mixed evenly throughout.

Wedging

Wedging is the process which mixes the clay evenly. This is carried out by cutting the clay block and bringing one half on top of the other. A strong table and cutting wire are essential.

Keep the clay block in a rectangular shape and try to work systematically so that all the clay is banged in turn.

▲ Wedging clay. The block is cut in two pieces and one is brought swiftly down onto the other to mix evenly.

Start with a block about 2–4 kg weight. This process can also be used for softening or stiffening clay by slicing it into layers and sandwiching it with softer (or harder) clay. Grog and sand is mixed in by the same sandwiching method.

Wrong way   **Right way**

Lifting heavy weights

Most of us are conscious of our backs at some time. It is better to lift properly and avoid back trouble; the golden rule is always to keep your back straight and bend your legs, whether you are tying shoe laces or lifting 25 kg. Also, if you are not used to lifting heavy weights, do it slowly and carefully rather than rush and have an accident.

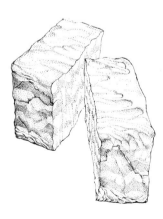

Kneading

When thoroughly wedged, the clay is kneaded to remove air bubbles. Here, practice is essential.

Start with a smallish lump of about 2 kg in weight, and use the ox-head method illustrated. Hold the clay lump on the top corners, and lift it towards you and twist it at the same time.

Move your hands round the block and repeat the movement. This process is similar to kneading bread dough but aims to remove rather than add air.

▶ The ox-head method of kneading. All clay preparation is best done steadily and thoroughly to avoid tiring oneself out.

▼ Blocks of clay showing the shapes obtained by ox-head kneading (right) and spiral kneading (left).

A second method known as spiral kneading is favoured by Oriental potters. The result, illustrated, shows the sort of shape which comes from this process. Again, the clay is held with both hands but the lifting is accompanied by a clockwise twist.

Clay is usually kneaded about 100 times. This may take 10 minutes or more, but do not hurry this stage.

Working states

Some clay is more suitable wetter and some is better drier. Illustrated below is a simple test to check whether or not the clay is hard or soft. As a general guide, clay which is sticky is too wet (**1**); it cracks and splits when too dry (**2**); when right it is clean and handlable (**3**). With experience you will be able to recognize these stages without testing.

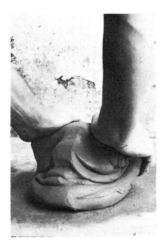

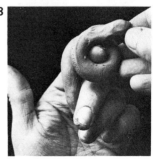

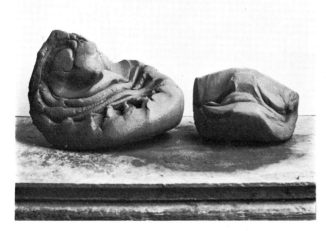

Experiments with clay

As a first introduction to what clay can do, a few experiments will reveal many of the mysteries of this marvellous material. Using a few simple tools, most of which are available in the home, quite pleasing results can be quickly obtained. Naturally, the greater the care taken, the better will be your result.

Flat dishes

Press a lump of prepared clay on to a sheet of newspaper or a cloth (this stops the clay sticking to the table surface) until it is fairly flat. Then roll it out with a rolling pin; turning the clay over will enable an even slab to be made. Aim to make it about 5 mm thick.

Cut out a shape from the slab, either freely or using a template, and fold up the sides to form a flat dish. Pinch any overlapping walls together to make a strong join and to keep up the sides. This will be particularly necessary with round shapes.

Clays at various states of hardness or softness will give different results. The best dishes are usually the neatest.

A second method of making flat dishes is to press small pellets of clay into a basin or bowl which has

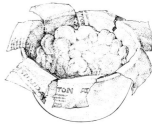

been lined with strips of newspaper. Start at the bottom and build up the sides. The pattern left by the pellets gives a pleasant decorative effect. As the clay dries, it shrinks from the walls and the pot can be lifted out and the newspaper removed.

Cutting and carving

These experiments are based on the use of the cutting wire, which often leaves pleasant textured surfaces. A ball or a square block of clay can be cut with the wire into several pieces and some ingenious interlocking shapes can result. These have no direct purpose other than to divert or amuse.

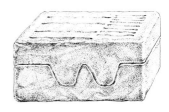

Forms cut with a wire

The inside of cut shapes can be hollowed out with a loop-ended modelling tool to make decorative boxes. Hard and soft clays will en-able different shapes to be cut, and additions to the body of sand or grog will give attractive textured surfaces.

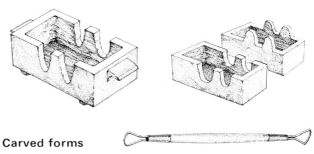

Carved forms

A chess set

Clay cut with a wire can be used to make a chess set. In the one illustrated, square blocks were cut all of the same thickness. The difference between the pieces was obtained by varying the height and by adding some simple form of decoration to the top.

Square lengths of the same thickness can be cut from a block of clay with a wire using a wooden guide at the side to determine the thickness.

Modelled decoration can be carved with a knife on top of the pieces, or more clay can be added to give designs in relief. Contrasting colours can be achieved by either using different coloured clays or by glazes.

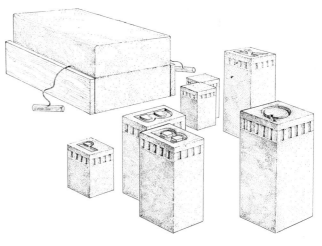

Making a moulded shape

The technique of forming shapes in moulds has long been in use. Moulds could be bird's nests in which clay has been smeared or can be made from plaster of Paris. For the beginner, the moulds must have simple shapes from which the pot can be easily removed. The basic technique involved is pressing soft plastic clay inside an easily made former or mould to retain its shape.

Tools

Some tools are essential, though many of these can be improvised. The rolling pin can come from the kitchen, but a length of plastic drainpipe will be just as good, provided it is long enough. Also required are a sharp, thin bladed knife and a metal straight edge.

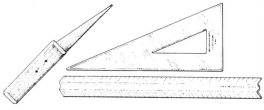

Strips of wood serve as thickness guides for rolling out the clay; sets 6 mm 9 mm and 12 mm thick allow a good variety of slabs to be made. Slabs can either be rolled out on newspaper, card or cloth. Material with a coarse texture such as hessian gives an attractive pattern.

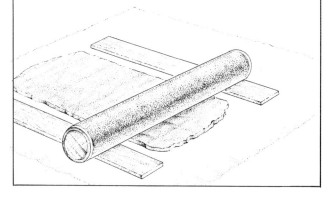

Method

First, well-prepared medium soft clay is pressed onto the rolling surface, and rolled level using the rolling guides. This flat slab of clay can now be laid into any suitable mould.

A simple mould can be made from strips of wood about 15 mm thick and 150 mm long, laid to form a square. Cut a 175 mm square from the slab of clay and lay it over the wooden square so that the inside takes the form of a flat dish. Gentle pressure on the inside with a damp sponge will alter the form.

Instead of strips of wood, the support walls could be made from stiff clay; alternatively a thick coil of clay bent to form a circle could equally well act as former for round flat dishes.

Hammock moulds

For larger dishes hammock moulds serve well. A length of fairly soft material suspended on the inside of a box or for round shapes, the inside of a bowl, is a method of improvising a mould. Depending on the curvature of the material, either deep or shallow dishes will result.

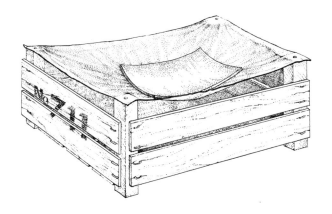

(slurry). Press the foot or foot ring firmly into position and carefully weld the join with the fingers. This will ensure a firm bond which will not open or crack.

Dishes made in a mould can look very handsome if the inside only is glazed and the unglazed body acts as a "frame" for the richly coloured or textured glaze.

Filling the mould

To fill the mould cut the shape you require in the clay while it is still a flat slab, as it is very much easier at this stage, and transfer it carefully to the mould. When the shape has become leather-hard, remove it from the mould but do not move it too soon or it will distort.

The edge can be decorated with an incised pattern or applied relief decoration.

Feet or a foot ring can be fitted at this stage. Mark on the bottom where the join is to be made, taking care to place the support centrally. Score the surface with a knife and paint on a mixture of clay and water

▲ Flat slabs of clay lend themselves to many forms of decoration. Here, leaves and twigs have been rolled onto the soft clay.

Decoration

One of the attractions of this method of making dishes is that the clay slabs can be decorated while flat, which allows a wide variety of techniques to be used.

Impressed designs, using everyday objects such as nuts and bolts, wheel cogs, shells and almost any textured surface can be made.

Tiny pellets of clay can be added to give a simple relief decoration, but paint each pellet with slurry before pressing it into position to ensure a good bond. This decoration can be very effective if placed around

the edge of the dish to frame it.

Many plants and leaves, if gently rolled into the surface of the clay, will leave imprints which give decorative patterns.

Particular care should be paid to the edges of moulded dishes to prevent them looking messy. This is often difficult to avoid when handling clay which is fairly soft. A pattern made by pressing a tool into the edge will help to overcome this problem. This was a technique used by many traditional country potters on their moulded dishes.

Slab pots

Various methods of making and using slabs of clay to make dishes have been referred to. This chapter explains how to use slabs to build up pots in a sort of ceramic carpentery. One of the chief advantages of this method is that it is a technique which enables pots with sharp, square edges to be made—a quality which has attracted potters for hundreds of years, especially those in the Far East. Boxes for cutlery or cigarettes and butter dishes can easily be made by this method.

Tools

When many slabs are required, they can more quickly be cut than rolled, though either method will serve. To cut slabs a cutting harp will be required; this is a piece of rigid metal with a taut wire stretched across it. Alternatively, two lengths of wood with notches cut at regular intervals, such as 5 mm, can be used to hold the wire.

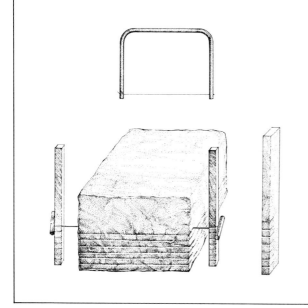

Preparing slabs

The clay is first well wedged and knocked into a block, as symmetrical as possible so that the length and width are approximately those of the required size of slabs.

Stand the block on a smooth even surface. Hold the harp firmly with both hands and either push or pull it through the block. Lift off the clay and remove the slab.

The method for using the wooden strips with the wire is similar except that the wire can be moved up a notch each time so that the entire block is eventually cut into slices. Leave the slabs to become leather-hard before cutting or building.

Slab building

First, design the shape you wish to make and cut templates of each part in stiffish card.

There are one or two basic rules to remember. Always stand the walls on the base so that as the pot contracts the base pulls in the walls; in this way, no splitting will occur.

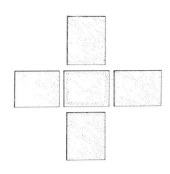

When cutting the slabs, place the rule on the template; this keeps it in position and prevents the knife slipping onto the part you want. Hold the knife vertically and draw it towards you two or three times until the cut is completed. To cut the slab in one movement requires great pressure and is likely to lead to distortion.

Joining the slabs

Score the surfaces which are to be joined and paint them with slurry. When placing sections in position, gently rock them so that the two surfaces get a good bite and a strong join is formed. Surplus slurry should just ooze out of the crack. The join can be further strengthened by ad-

ding a thin coil of clay on the inside and smoothing it in with the fingers or a wooden modelling tool.

Support the upright walls with bricks or blocks of wood while joining, and allow the finished piece to dry slowly, perhaps covered with a sheet of polythene. The outside joins can be cleaned off, using a wooden modelling tool or a piece of hacksaw blade.

Joins can either be made at right angles or can be mitred at an angle of 45°. Whichever method you choose, take this into account when working out the size of the templates, as this is affected by the thickness of the clay.

Cutting the slabs

When leatherhard, the slabs can be cut to size without distortion. Allow the slabs to dry slowly in a draught-free place and turn them frequently as this will help to keep them flat. Drying can be safely speeded up by placing the slabs between two asbestos batts. However, remember that all slabs which are to be joined must be at the same state, otherwise they may crack and split apart.

Rolling round a former

Once some experience of using and handling clay slabs has been gained, the scope for experiment and ingenuity is almost boundless. Using slabs as ceramic carpentry enables square corners to be made, but soft slabs can be manipulated and handled to form pots with rounded, more gentle corners. Only with practice will you be able to judge at what stage your slabs can best be handled. This is especially true when using a former.

Method

Basically, this technique involves using a former around which clay slabs are wrapped until they have stiffened sufficiently to bear their own weight without distorting. This is slightly more difficult than it sounds; if the clay is too soft it will wrap round without cracking, but can be messed up very easily. If the clay slab stiffens too much it will not wrap round without cracking at the corners. Catching the clay at the correct moment is therefore critical. The second danger point is to remove the former at the right point, for as the clay dries it shrinks onto the former and will crack unless freed.

The clay slabs can either be rolled out or sliced by any of the methods described so far. Round supports such

as jars, cardboard tubes or square formers such as wooden blocks and tins can be used, so long as they can be easily removed. Always wrap the former in newspaper as this prevents sticking. Depending on the size of your pot, the clay can either be wrapped round, or rolled over the former. Cut the shape first. Join by scoring and applying slurry and press and weld as usual.

Fix the base last of all;

stand the walls on a slab slightly larger than required, join by the usual method and trim away any surplus clay. Illustrated below is a variety of shapes which can be made easily by wrapping clay around a former. As experience is gained, lips and/or handles can be added and pots can be joined together to form such things as garden pots or pot-holders, desk tidies and so on.

Incised and relief decoration look well on these strong, simple shapes.

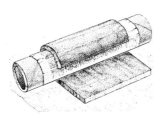

◄ Four ways of using slabs of clay are shown in this group of modern studio pots. All have been fired to stoneware temperature except the front left round pot which is earthenware.

Pinch pots

The pleasures of handling clay direct can be enjoyed to the full by pinching out a small clay lump to form a pot. No tools are necessary and the immediateness of the technique is particularly useful for finding out about the many qualities of clay. However, the directness of the technique belies the skill necessary to make a successful pot. Co-ordination between hand and eye and correct judgement of pressure take time to develop, so if your first pots collapse be reassured that this happens to most beginners. If this does happen, try using softer or harder clay.

Preparation

Use medium soft, well-prepared clay and begin with small lumps of about 50 grams, not much bigger than a golf ball. Make the balls as even and regular as you can without handling them too much. The heat from your hands has a tendency to dry out the surface of the clay and cause it to crack.

If this happens you are spending too long on one piece. Try to work more quickly. Alternatively you can just moisten your hands with water (not the clay) which should counteract it.

Method

Hold the clay ball in your left hand and gently press your right thumb down the centre, leaving about 5 mm at the base. To make the walls, lightly squeeze the clay between your thumb on the inside and your fingers on the outside, forcing the clay upwards and outwards.

Rotate the pot in your hand as you work. Try to use equal pressure all around otherwise the pot becomes

1

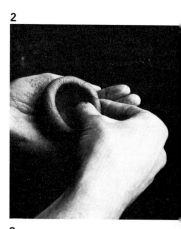

2

3

lopsided and difficult to handle. As you work try placing your hands and fingers in different positions until you find those which suit you best. There is no correct method—it is up to you to find the one which works best for you.

Keep the rim slightly thicker than you finally require; this helps to prevent it cracking as well as helping to keep a bowl shape. It can be thinned later if necessary. Aim to make the walls the same thickness all round. Some potters like to make these small pots with walls as thin as egg or coconut shells.

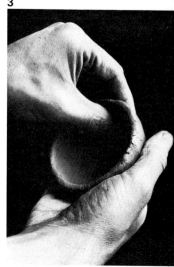

Larger pots

When you find you can manage the small balls try slightly larger ones; tennis ball size is quite big for a pinch pot. With a larger lump you may have to work in a slightly different way. If the pot gets too floppy, it may be necessary to re-start.

However easy these little hand pots look, they need much care and patience to achieve a sensitive, well-balanced effort. Some potters rest their pots on a sponge to stiffen slightly before working on them again. Thin, delicate walls can be achieved by paring away the clay with a hack-saw blade until it is eggshell thin.

Decoration

Small, delicate pinch pots need appropriate decoration, so the advice here is to go

4

carefully. A foot welded to the pot gives it an extra special look, though this must be kept in proportion.

Pinch pots of the same size can be joined together rim to rim to make solid looking eggs which can be used as decorative paper weights, or they can be converted into animals or figures. Spherical pots can also be made by this method.

To make bowls with in-cised decoration, pinhole patterns or painted designs can be used. The scope is large for the imaginative potter.

Other pots can be given a smooth "burnished" or shiny surface. Do this at the leatherhard stage by rubbing the pot with a smooth tool or pebble. This compresses the particles of clay and gives them a dull shine which will remain on the pot unless covered over by glaze.

Delicate, light designs can be scratched into the burnished surface with great effect but, as usual, the best advice is not to overdo the decoration. An understated small delicate pot which is pleasant to handle is a very good achievement.

Below is a selection of pinch pots waiting to be fired.

5

Coil pots

Of all the pottery-making techniques, coiling is the most versatile. Pieces can be almost any size from small egg cups to huge wine and oil containers or cider jars. Shapes too can range from beautiful, round symmetrical forms to ovals, squares, rectangles or any combination. Sometimes the variety is bewildering, as are the various ways in which coil pots can be made. Basically the technique consists of building coils or rings of clay on top of each other and joining them together to form walls. The method described here is a useful one which can be adapted for individual needs.

1

2

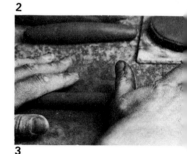

3

Method

Make the base first by pressing or rolling clay to about 10 mm thickness. Cut out the shape and size you want, either using a template or by spinning the wheel and scoring with a knife.

To roll the coils, you need a fairly large table space with plenty of room for movement. First squeeze out thickish and even lengths of clay, about 25 mm in diameter. Taper the ends so

Tools

Few tools are required because, as usual, the fingers are the most versatile and useful. Some sort of batt support is required to build the pot on, and a turntable or banding wheel will make coiling much quicker.

4

5

6

coils your pot may seem floppy in which case leave it to stiffen slightly. Remember that you cannot join coils to leatherhard clay, so do not let the clay edge get too dry if you want to carry on building.

Once the shape has been built, the surface can either be left with finger marks or be smoothed off. This is done by pulling the rough side of a hacksaw blade diagonally across the coils. The teeth marks can be smoothed over with the back edge of the blade.

that as the coils are rolled air is not trapped in the ends.

Roll the coils using the whole length of your hands and keep them parallel to the surface of the table. Start in the middle of the coil and move outwards. For a pot about 30 cm tall, the coils need to be about 10 mm in diameter. Lay the first coil just inside the edge of the base, flatten the end and press it on carefully. Smooth the outside and inside of the coil onto the base. Add the next coil and join and repeat the process until about six coils have been joined.

At this stage check the shape for evenness; correct it by gently pushing from the inside or tapping from the outside. After several

▶ A Nigerian stoneware pot, hand-built with coils of clay and decorated with a traditional Nigerian incised pattern.

Decorating with slip

The idea of using different coloured clays for decoration on pots is one which seems almost as old as pottery itself. However, the careful preparation and application of liquid clay slips coloured with colouring oxides is a technique which was developed to a fine art in Britain in the 17th and 18th centuries. Slipware potters trailed and poured the coloured slips onto the leatherhard pots with swiftness and skill to give rich decorative patterns which are greatly admired today.

Tools

Certain tools are essential for slip trailing. The slip trailers themselves need a fine nozzle and a flexible rubber or plastic bulb. A suitable tool is an enema syringe, which can be bought from your local chemist. A plastic tall bottle fitted with a rubber nozzle such as an inner tube valve rubber will also work. For preparing the slip, two buckets, an 80-mesh sieve, sieving sticks and a stiff brush are required.

Slip recipes

In the recipes the main ingredients should add up to 100. Colouring ingredients are added to this amount.

Red slip

Red clay	100

White slip

Feldspar	20
Ball clay	25
China clay	35
Flint	20

Black slip

Red clay	100
Iron oxide	6
Manganese oxide	3
Cobalt oxide	2

Preparing the slip

Weigh the ingredients, add them to water and leave to soak for about twelve hours. Mix thoroughly and pass twice through the sieve. Slip should have the consistency of double cream and if the slip is allowed to settle, surplus water can be removed. Always stir the slip well before use.

The easiest way to apply slip is to dip leatherhard

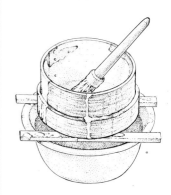

pots. Hold the pots vertically upside down and gently lower them into the slip. Try not to get slip on the inside. If you want to slip the inside and outside, do the inside first and let this dry before doing the outside. Remember that freshly dipped pots soften and need careful handling.

Pouring slip

Slip can also be poured on the outside of pots to give apron-like decorative effects.

Trailing
Slip trailing is great fun and once you have confidence you will enjoy it. Use slightly thicker slip and stir well. Fill the trailer with slip and practise first on the bench top. Keep the nozzle slightly above the surface so the slip flows out. Decoration can be trailed onto leatherhard surfaces or onto surfaces covered with fresh slip, in which case the decoration sinks in and lies flat. Traditional designs include "feathering", in which

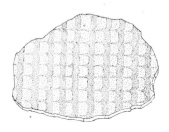

lines of slip are laid side by side and a bristle pulled across.

Slip decoration can be done on flat clay slabs which when leatherhard can be used for any of the building techniques so far described.

Two methods
There are basically two sorts of slip decoration: wet on wet, or wet on dry. In the first method, slip is decorated while still wet, either by pulling a comb or your fingers across it, or by trailing on different coloured slip which sinks into the wet slip. In the second method, stiff slip is trailed or piped onto a dry (leatherhard) clay. This is the method used by the Toft family (page 18). Experiment with both methods to see the sort of effects you can get.

Traditionally, slip decoration is associated with earthenware and few potters use the technique today. This is a pity as it is a relatively simple method which gives rich and attractive results.

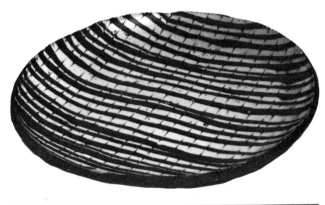

Letters
Slip trailing on a leatherhard surface can be an effective and pleasing method of decoration.

In this example the letters or figures were cut out of thick slabs of clay and a decoration of coloured slips piped on in dots and lines.

If you are going to fix these figures to the wall, remember to cut screw holes in the clay when it is leatherhard.

Coloured clay and its uses

Different coloured clays occur in nature, for example red terracotta and cream-coloured earthenware, but a wider range of colours can be obtained by adding a suitable body stain to a light coloured clay. Agate ware is the name given to pots made from different coloured clays partially blended together so that when the surface is cleaned the different colours show clearly. Earthenware is the most suitable temperature at which to work, as a wider range of bright colours can be obtained. At stoneware temperatures, the colour range tends to be darker and more limited.

Mixing in the colour

Colour is added in the form of powdered body stain, bought from a supplier, which is mixed into a light-coloured earthenware body. Amounts of up to 10–15 per cent of body stain can be added, smaller quantities will give paler colours.

Weigh out fairly soft clay and body stain. Slice the clay and poke some small amounts of stain into each slice until it is all mixed in. Wedge and knead the clay until the colour is distributed evenly throughout the lump.

Marbled clay

Marbled clay is made by sandwiching thin slices of coloured clay and partially kneading the lump.

Mix only coloured clays of the same consistency together, otherwise they dry unevenly and may crack. Too much kneading will mix the colours together completely. You can check this by slicing a corner with a wire.

Striped clay

With the wire, slice the coloured clay you want and sandwich the slices of different colours in any arrangement you wish. Carefully roll one slice onto the other so that no air is trapped in between. Build up the block evenly as it will not be

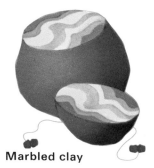

Marbled clay

wedged or kneaded. Then cut across the slices to get slabs of striped clay.

Square patterned clay

Knock blocks of the coloured clay you want to use into even regular squares. Slice them with the wire resting on the notched wooden sticks as shown on page 42. Carefully turn this cut block on its side so that the cuts now run vertical, and slice the block again. This will result in cube shaped lengths

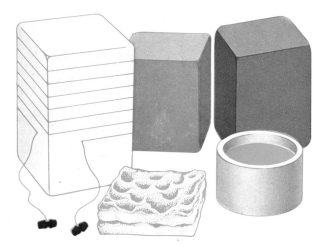

Striped clay

as shown in the illustration. Assemble the lengths to form a block of clay with the squares in any desired colour pattern.

Other patterns

Once the principle of colouring clay and putting it together has been understood, many variations can be tried. For example, sandwiches of clays can be rolled round and joined together. The possible permutations of colour and arrangement are numerous.

Using coloured clays

Any of the working methods of making pots described in this section can be used with coloured clays. For example, pinch pots can be made from two or three coloured clays banged to-

Cubed clay

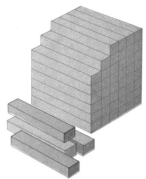

gether to form a ball. As the clay is worked, different colours will come to the surface in irregular patterns. Slab pots, coil pots and moulded pots all lend themselves to this process and coloured clays can also be moulded on the wheel.

Finishing off pots

The surface of pots made out of coloured clays is often smudgy and only when this is cleaned is the pattern of the clays revealed. Do this when the pot is bone dry: with a piece of fine wire wool gently rub the surface. To prevent the dust blowing about let it drop into a bowl of water. As you clean, the pattern will emerge. Finish the pot with a transparent glaze.

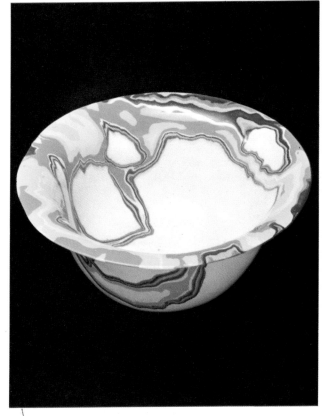

◄ A small earthenware bowl made by Paul Philp. It is made from different coloured clays assembled in layers, laid inside a hollow mould and finished with a clear transparent glaze. The colours were obtained by adding body stain to white earthenware.

Press-moulded pots

Moulds made out of plaster were not in widespread use until comparatively recently and represent a large step forward in ceramic technology. They enable the potter to design and make almost any shape and fill it. The moulds and formers described earlier limit the scope of the potter, but plaster moulds enlarge the possibilities. These pages describe how to make a one-piece drop-out mould and fill it by using flat slabs of clay. These dishes can be made singly or in sets.

Making the mould

First, make a solid model of the shape you require out of ungrogged clay. Start with a fairly simple shape and make a template in cardboard of its base shape. Build up the solid clay on this. Bear in mind that the final pot will have shrunk 8–10 per cent. A simple oval or square is a good starting shape—about 20 cm wide and 50 mm deep. Make the sides slope inwards. Finally, smooth the clay sides with a hacksaw blade before casting. It is worth spending time getting your model correct as imperfections will be picked up in the plaster cast.

Lay the model on a sheet of glass and build walls round it, 50 mm from the model and 75 mm above the highest point of the model. The walls can be clay or wood, lino or perspex. Seal all the joins with clay. Mix the plaster of Paris according to the instructions on page 34; it is better to mix slightly too much rather than too little plaster.

Pour the plaster as it is just setting over the model to a depth of 50 mm above the top. When the plaster has set fairly hard (in about two hours), remove the model from the inside.

Throw away any clay contaminated with plaster, as this will melt if used in the kiln and spoil good work. Any rough edges on the mould can be smoothed with a rough file or surform blade, but be careful not to damage the edges. Let the mould dry out thoroughly for about a week before use.

How the plaster mould is made

Filling the mould

Slabs for filling the mould can be prepared by any of the previously described methods. The slab must be laid inside the mould while still soft, otherwise it will crack as it is eased into position. To place it inside the mould, cut the clay to approximately the right size, support it over the outstretched hand and lower it into the mould. Gently push in the edges to ensure that the whole of the mould is

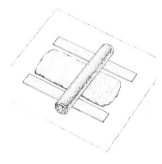

filled. A damp sponge can be used to push the clay down from the inside, but be careful not to make dents in the slab as these cannot be smoothed out.

When this has been completed, the edges can be trimmed. Hold a wire level on top of the mould at right angles to the wall as illustrated. The cut edge should be left clean by the wire and this can be further smoothed by passing your

Decoration

Once the dish is in the mould, many sorts of decorative techniques can be used. Slip trailed decoration is effective.

First, a layer of slip is

▲ Press-moulded pots. The square earthenware dish was made in a shallow mould; the oval dish was moulded more

finger over it. Alternatively this edge can be rounded by sponging it, using long firm strokes. Short strokes will leave a nobbly, uncertain edge. A modelling tool can be used to make a simple but effective impressed design which acts as a pleasant frame for the dish.

poured inside and the surplus poured away. The edge of the dish should now be wiped clean of slip. Trail on the desired design, but remember that slip tends to move on sloping surfaces.

freely. The stoneware round pot was made in two halves which were luted together when leatherhard.

The wheel: an intro- duction

Throwing is the technique used to make pots on the fast spinning potter's wheel, and a skilled potter makes it seem an effortless and easy process. The art of the potter, however, is achieved only by practice. If you have no success when you first start to throw on the wheel, remember that it is only with patience and practice that you will acquire the art. When you practise, short, frequent sessions are more useful than long sessions at irregular intervals.

Throwing

No book can replace the words of advice from a skilled teacher, nor can it match the value of actually watching a potter at work.

What a book can do, however, is to point out the major steps involved in the throwing process and act as a useful reference point when looking at the potter at work. Here, all the basic throwing, turning and finishing processes are described and illustrated.

◀ The throwing chapters of the activity section describe how all these pots can be made, beginning with the plain cylinder and ending with the soup tureen. All have been fired to stoneware temperature (1260°C). The jug has a brown tenmoku glaze (page 77). The flat dish is decorated with oxide colours painted onto the unfired glaze. The ladle inside the tureen is made by luting a small thrown bowl onto a long pulled handle at the leatherhard stage.

The electric wheel

There are basically two sorts of wheel, the electric and the kickwheel. The electric wheel is driven by an electric motor, the speed of which is usually controlled by a foot pedal or lever.

A good electric wheel has a slow, even, steady speed which can be quickly increased as necessary. Modern wheels are light in weight and are capable of carrying quite heavy lumps of clay without loss of torque. This is one of the advantages of the electric wheel. They are also fitted with sensitive controls which allow freedom and flexibility.

Prices for a good electric wheel start at around £200, cheaper wheels can be bought, though they usually have less sensitive controls and are unable to carry large amounts of clay. For the beginner, the electric wheel is ideal. It enables full concentration to centre on the throwing, and is far less tiring than the kickwheel. Do ensure that the wiring complies with accepted standards, and if necessary check this with a qualified electrician.

The kickwheel

The kickwheel is slower to work on; the wheel is fitted with a heavy fly wheel which is either moved around by a crank and treadle arrangement (like the English kick wheel) or is kicked round directly with the foot (the continental wheel). Both are operated from a sitting position. It is almost impossible to stand and kick and throw pots at the same time.

The advantages of the kickwheel are its silence and the intimate control it allows over the wheel speed. The action of the leg and the throwing process become automatic in time and enable the slightest or greatest speed change without thought. Prices for kickwheels start at around £70.

Whichever wheel a potter chooses is a matter of personal preference. One is not better than the other; it depends very much on which one suits your working method.

Throwing technique

Throwing has been described as being like the skill of the wrestler rather than the boxer—more a question of putting pressure in the right places than of sheer strength.

The basic principle of throwing is the use of pressure against the radius of the spinning centrifugal force of the clay. All pressure is directed at the centre of the clay—if this is not achieved, the clay goes off-centre and becomes uneven.

Some potters prefer to throw with slurry, that is a mixture of clay and water; others prefer clean water. The use of either is best kept to a minimum; it is a bad throwing habit to keep flooding on water, as this weakens the clay and does not aid throwing.

The longer the time you spend throwing, the softer the clay will become. The quicker the throwing time, the stronger the pot. If your pot is difficult to lift off the wheel this may be because you have spent too long making it or you began with clay which was too soft. Speeding up the throwing process only becomes possible with practice, but it is an aim to be borne in mind.

Preparation

Always begin throwing by wedging and kneading your clay well. Even the most experienced potters find they cannot work with badly wedged clay; for example, air bubbles which suddenly appear in the wall of a pot may ruin it.

Weigh out your clay lumps so that you get to know how large a pot a particular amount can make. Weigh out six lumps to begin with and keep the lumps wrapped up in polythene to prevent them drying out until you use them.

Allow your pots to dry slowly as this enables the process to be even; it is a good idea to put them inside tins or an air-tight cupboard (a damp cupboard). Avoid leaving them where draughts will dry out the rim or one side as this leads to warped forms.

Tools

The thrower's tools are very personal, and chosen very much as extensions of the hands and fingers. Essential tools are a fine natural sponge, a twisted cutting wire (this can be made by twisting together two strands of wire), a bowl of water, a sponge tied to a stick for mopping out narrow-necked pots and a wooden tool for cleaning the bottom of pots. For turning or trimming, a metal tool is required: this can be made from a length of metal banding wire bent to form a triangle, with a handle about 100 mm long.

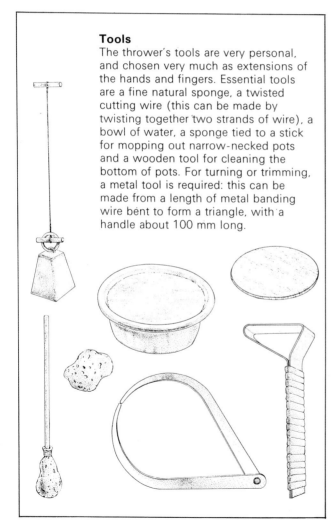

◄ This photograph shows a potter at work on an English kickwheel. The treadle is kicked with the left foot. The kickwheel is more difficult to work than the electric wheel, but it is also more sensitive to changes in speed.

▼ This ceramic tile, made in the 19th century, shows a potter throwing on a wheel. He has two assistants, a bench boy and a boy to turn the wheel for him.

How to throw a cylinder

at work. This is the best way to learn how to use a wheel. Notice where the hands hold the clay, and try to practise these movements.

1. Tools needed are lifting scraper, sponge and wire. Weigh lumps of prepared clay into 0.5 kg balls and sharply throw one onto the middle of the wheelhead. Push it into the centre if necessary.

Above all, take any opportunity to watch a potter

2. Establish a good wheel speed (anti-clockwise), wet your hands and wrap them round the clay. Use water sparingly throughout. Gradually increase the pressure until the clay is moving evenly and a tall shape is formed.

3. Wrap the left hand round the clay and hold the right hand over the top. Press down on the corner towards the centre of the clay and form a round shape.

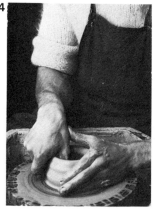

4. Once on centre open up the clay with the right thumb, going first down the middle, then across the bottom to form the base.

5. Bring up the walls by pulling up rolls of clay with the fingers of the right hand outside and the left hand inside.

6. Repeat this until a cylinder about 130 mm tall is made. Keep the rim rounded rather than flat.

7. Alternative sorts of rim can be made. This one is thickened and will later be turned into a jug.

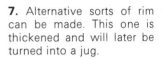

8. When finished, the pot is removed from the wheel. Flood clean water onto the wheelhead and pass the wire underneath.

9. The pot can be lifted off with the scraper and put on a smooth flat surface to become leatherhard.

61

10. The bottom and sides of the cylinder are now trimmed or turned. Fix the leatherhard pot centrally on the wheel-head with clay.

Flat dishes

10

11

Thrown pottery can be generally divided into two sorts: hollow ware and flat ware. Hollow ware, as its name implies, includes shapes which are usually tall and contain space; a cylinder is the obvious example. In contrast, flat ware contains little or no space and includes articles such as plates and dishes. For throwing, two different techniques are required, especially in the early stages when the clay is being centred and opened out. For a cylinder, the centred clay will resemble a squat mushroom with the "stalk" being the width of the cylinder; the top part is thrown to become the walls. With flat dishes, the clay is centred into a concave shape which is then opened up with the ball of the hand.

11. The sides are trimmed with a turning tool made of metal banding wire. A good wheel speed is necessary.

1

When making any flat shapes it is important to compress the clay on the bottom to prevent it from warping during the firing. Clay used in the walls is compressed during the throwing process, but special attention has to be paid to the base to ensure that it is thrown solid.

12. Finally the base is turned, leaving a neat foot-ring on the edge. Smooth off any sharp corners with your finger.

2

12

1. Weigh out 500 gram lumps from slightly harder clay than that used for cylinders. Centre by squeezing the clay up and pressing down. When centred the clay is opened by the ball of the right hand, using the left hand to control the spread of the clay.

2. Rudimentary walls are now formed. The base determines the total width of the pot: about 125 mm. The walls are pulled up by the same process as for a cylinder.

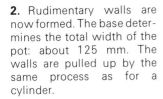

3. The base on any flat dish must be compressed to make it flat and even, as well as to strengthen it generally. This is achieved by pressing the thumb across the base. Repeat this movement two or three times.

4. After the walls have been brought up they can be completed by using a smooth wooden modelling tool held against the walls. From the amount of clay used here, a dish about 125 mm x 25 mm will be made. Finish off the rim with the fingers.

5. When the sides have been made smooth, an incised line made with a wooden tool can give useful definition to the shape.

6. The finished pot can be removed from the wheelhead with the scraper, though a dish which is 125 mm wide is about the widest size which can be removed by this method. When leatherhard, the dish is turned by the same method as that described for a cylinder.

63

Throwing bowls

Of the more simple shapes, bowls are perhaps the ones which demand greatest sensitivity and awareness of the qualities of clay; a good bowl is well-balanced, not too heavy or too light in weight, and the walls are of even thickness with no lumps or bulges. The illustration on the right shows a variety of shapes which can be tried. The one on the left suggests enclosed space, the one in the centre a growing shape and the one on the right is a "cosy" form. Each type is useful for different purposes.

1. The method of making a bowl lies halfway between that used for a cylinder and that used for a flat dish. The centred clay (weighing here about 500 gram) is opened with the thumb to leave a funnel shape with a rounded bottom.

2. The walls are pulled up leaving a good thickness of clay at the top. This can later be stretched to form

2

the diameter of the bowl. Do not pull out too quickly or the clay may be stretched and split.

3. As the bowl grows, more clay should be brought up from the base. Generally speaking, the width at the base should be about one-third that of the diameter at the top. Try to keep the inside of the bowl a smooth, flowing and continuous line.

1

3

Suggested shapes for bowls

4

5

4. Pay particular attention to the rim and use the fingers to remove any surplus slurry The final movements should extend the bowl to its fullest size.

5. Mop out any surplus water from the inside with a fine sponge, then go over the surface with the ends of the fingers. This removes any sponge marks and smooths over any grog or sand

brought to the surface by the sponge. Remove the pot with the scraper as usual.

6. When leatherhard, the bowl is put back on the wheel and trimmed. Aim to make the walls the same thickness throughout. On this bowl a fairly deep footring is cut which gives a pleasant lift to the pot. Try making bowls of various shapes.

6

Lidded jars

1. For this straightforward cylindrical jar 500 gram of clay is used. The finished jar is about 150 mm tall and 90 mm wide. Use clay slightly stiffer than usual. Centre and open the clay up as for making the cylinder but leave a good roll of clay at the top from which the seating can be made. Make the seating about halfway through the throwing process by pressing the forefinger of the left hand into the roll of clay at the rim.

2. Continue throwing the cylinder until it is completed. Then finish off the gallery, which should be sufficiently generous to allow a good seating for the lid. Again using the left forefinger, press the back of the nail across the gallery. Leave the actual rim rounded and quite thick so that it gives a strong finish to the shape. Measure the width with a ruler or calipers. Remove the pot by the usual method and trim when leatherhard.

1

2

Different types of lid

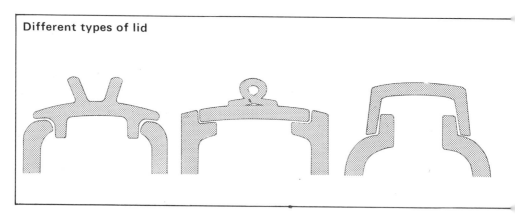

The lid

1. Weigh a 100 gram clay lump, using clay in the same state as that used for the pot. Centre and open up, leaving clay in the centre to form the knob. For small amounts of

clay, centring is easier if a fast wheel speed is maintained during the early stages.

2. Continue opening up. Leave a good roll of clay for the edges.

3. The lid should be almost formed. The edge is thrown across the fingers of the right hand, and the knob is shaped.

4. The rim of the lid should be rounded to sit snugly in the gallery seating. Check the diameter with the calipers or rule. If it is too big, trim with a wire. To turn the bottom of the lid, stand it upside down in the jar placed and held on the wheel.

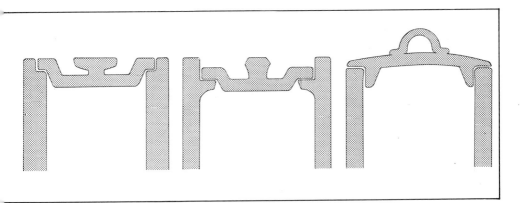

Lips and handles

Lips

1. Lips are made on jugs immediately they have been thrown. On this jug a thickened rim allows a generous lip. First pull up the rim with the thumb and fingers so that the spout is pointing upwards. This allows it a more upward thrust.

2. Supporting the clay with the moistened fingers, smooth down the lip as illustrated. As a general guide, make the lip too big at this stage as it still has to shrink considerably. Finally, smooth over with the finger when leatherhard.

Handles

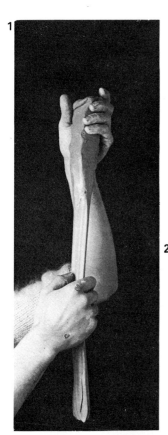

Handles

1. Pulled handles are made from stiff clay, cut into a long rectangle. Hold this at eye level and stroke it with the wet right hand to form a long strap which can be nipped off with the thumb. Try to get a slight taper in the thickness and an even width.

2. Lay the pulled handles on a wooden board to stiffen slightly before being added to the pot.

3. Score the pot with a knife and dab it with slip. Tap the widest end of the handle and, holding it firmly, press it onto the pot and smooth over the join.

4. Holding the pot horizontally, wet the right hand and smooth over the handle, stroking it even.

5. Lower the bottom end, press it firmly onto the jug and smooth on the edges.

How to make a soup tureen and bowls

All the throwing processes described so far will need to be mastered before this project can be attempted. Though in this sequence a 2 kg lump of clay was thrown, an adequate tureen can be made with a smaller amount. Large shapes cannot be lifted easily from the wheel but need to be thrown on a false wheelhead, called a batt, made of thick plywood or hard wood. This is attached to the wheelhead with clay and is lifted off afterwards with the pot still on it.

Fixing the batt
1. Centre and press flat a 600 gram lump of clay, using the side of the hand.

2. Cut rings into this at 25 mm intervals with a wooden tool and score a cross to prevent suction holding on the batt.

3. Place the batt onto the clay support, as centrally as possible. A sharp tap in the centre will fix it.

Throwing the tureen

6

4. Centre the clay and open up; with larger amounts of clay this process should be done slowly.

5. Bring up the walls fairly straight, but leave plenty of clay at the rim for seating.

6. Make the seating gallery for the lid half way through the process; press in the left forefinger and aim to make a good generous seating with a strong rounded rim.

7. Finish off the rounding of the shape last; mop and smooth out the inside, measure the diameter with calipers and pass a twisted wire underneath the tureen. Lift off the batt with the tureen still in position.

8

9

The lid
8. Throw the lid as for a flat bowl, leaving it rounded in the centre with a rounded rim.

9. Check the diameter with calipers and adjust as necessary. Pass a wire underneath and leave the lid to dry.

10

10. When leatherhard, turn the lid and throw a knob onto it or add a strap handle.

Soup bowls
11. Matching soup bowls can be made from 500 gram clay lumps. They are opened up as described for small bowls. Leave a good thickness at the base for a foot ring and make the first shape similar to a funnel. Gradually bring up the walls, but do not open them to their fullest diameter until the final throwing stages.

12. The last movements give the shape its final outward spread. Turn it when leatherhard and give it a footring.

11

12

Fixing the handles
13. Handles are pulled by the usual method. The width and thickness should be even throughout. Add the handles at the leatherhard stage after the turning has been completed. Score the surface of the pot, dab on slurry and press and weld on the ends of the handle.

▼ The finished soup tureen and bowls, fired to 1260°C with a dolomite matt glaze. The bowls are designed to stack easily.

The kiln and biscuit firing

Firing pots is the final stage of production. A bright, red-white heat is necessary to transform the dried clay into a pot, a heat far in excess of the average domestic oven. Pots can be fired in homemade kilns, but small electric kilns which operate off a 13 amp plug or cooker point can be purchased at moderate cost.

Your kiln

Pots can be fired at local evening classes but if you can afford your own kiln you will have greater control over the firing procedure. Kilns can be purchased in many sizes, but one with a 30 cm x 30 cm x 30 cm firing chamber is a modest and not too expensive start.

Be sure to get a qualified electrician to check that it is wired up correctly. Temperature in the kiln is measured with a thermocouple and a pyrometer, an electrical device that registers high temperatures.

Cones

Cones are also used to indicate temperature in the kiln. They are triangular-shaped pyramids, about 65 mm tall, that soften and bend at different temperatures according to their number. Staffordshire Cone 06, for example, falls over at 980°C, which is the average biscuit firing temperature; cones are supported in a wad of clay and placed in front of the spy hole in the door. At 980°C the cone will soften and fall over, indicating that the temperature has been reached.

Keep a kiln log of each firing. Record the time, the kiln control, and the temperature every hour. This will enable a regular check to be kept on how your firings are progressing.

Pots for the biscuit firing should be perfectly dry and fettled to remove any bits of clay. They can be packed inside or on top of one another so long as the weight is equally balanced.

Kiln furniture

▶ Kiln furniture should be kept clean and free of glaze splashes. Top left are three cones in a cone stand. In the bowl is a mixture of batt wash for painting onto kiln shelves. The three-cornered spur is for supporting earthenware pots and the castellated prop and tubular props are for building up kiln shelves.

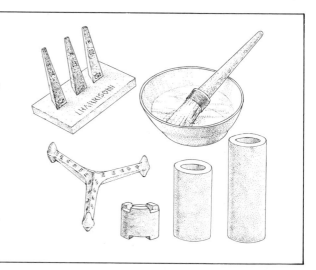

Firing schedule
1. 0°–200°C. low control setting, vent open.
2. 200°–500°C. medium control setting, vent open.
3. 500°–980°C. top control setting, vent closed.

1. Heat input regulator.
2. Light indicating that the kiln is working.
3. Heat fuse.
4. Electric heating elements.
5. Biscuit pots.
6. Vent with brick in position.
7. Pyrometer dial showing temperature inside kiln.
8. Spyhole for watching cones.

An electric kiln packed for biscuit firing

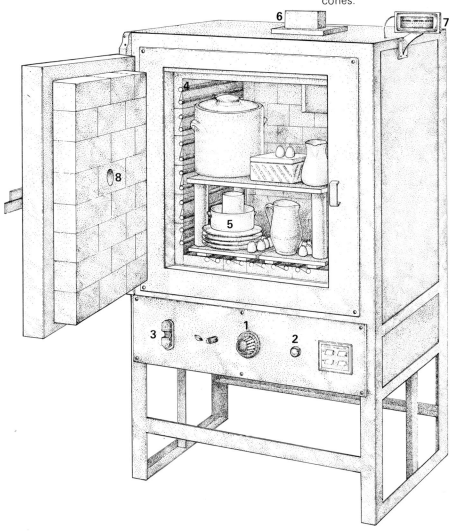

Glazes

Glaze can be applied to the biscuit fired pot in a variety of ways, each method having its own merits, but all aiming to give an even coating of glaze roughly 2 mm thick. Glaze can be applied by painting if it is mixed with a gum arabic solution which makes it dry to a non powdery surface. This method is useful when only a small amount of glaze is available. Spraying glaze requires complicated and expensive equipment. Pouring and dipping are the easiest and most useful methods.

Mixing glaze

Glazes can either be bought ready prepared from a pottery supplier, or they can be mixed according to known recipes. The experienced potter can work out glazes from a knowledge of different ingredients.

All manufactured glazes must be prepared and fired according to the instructions; they are usually supplied in powder form, added to water and passed through a sieve to remove any lumps.

A wide range of prepared coloured and textured glazes are available for stoneware and earthenware and this is a good way for the beginner to work with glaze.

Mixing your own glazes from recipes enables you to adjust the ingredients to get different results, and therefore have control over the process. For example, glazes can be made more matt by increasing the china clay content.

Five recipes for stoneware glazes are included here, and all can be altered according to the effect required. All the materials with which to mix these glazes can be bought from pottery suppliers, together with a free catalogue which gives some information on how the materials react in the glaze. These are excellent sources of handy information which are also useful for reference.

Mixing the glaze

To prepare the glaze carefully weigh out the ingredients and add them to water; this helps to prevent lumps forming. Stir up the mixture and pass it twice through an 80 mesh sieve. If the glaze is too thin let it stand and settle and then pour away some of the clear water from the top. Glaze generally needs to have the consistency of single cream.

Earthenware glaze recipes using a borax or an alkaline frit mixed with china clay or red clay in the approximate proportion 80–20 can be tried and from these simple mixtures workable glazes can be found. Always test them first on vertical tiles before putting them onto pots.

Make your own glazes

Working out your own glazes, is, perhaps, the most satisfying way of preparing glazes, and also the most difficult. First, test each glaze material, mixing it with water and painting it onto a piece of clay, to see how it behaves in the kiln. According to the results, mix two or three materials together, carefully noting and modifying the results. Useful starting materials are feldspar, whiting, china clay, flint and dolomite.

Poison

Most of the materials used in pottery are toxic if inhaled in large quantities or eaten. Simple common sense procedures will eliminate this risk. For example, dust down by wet wiping, do not eat while making pots, and mix any fire prepared glazes *only* as instructed. Avoid the use of lead glazes which under some circumstances can be poisonous when fired.

◄ The glazes illustrated here were applied by dipping and were fired to 1260°C (Staffordshire cone H8A) in an electric kiln.

1 Clear transparent
Potash feldspar	42
Ball clay	20
Whiting	15
Flint	23

2 Matt textured
Feldspar	40
China clay	15
Ball clay	20
Whiting	14
Flint	11

3 Smooth white
Feldspar	62
Dolomite	20
China clay	18

4 Black brown tenmoku
Cornish stone	56
Whiting	14
China clay	6
Ball clay	4
Flint	20
Red iron oxide	9

5 Green speckled wax
Feldspar	53
Barium carbonate	21
China clay	10
Flint	6
Whiting	10
Copper carbonate	1.5

The colours of any of the above glazes can be changed by the addition of colouring oxides.

How to apply glaze

After the biscuit firing, the pots are covered in glaze before being fired a second time in the glaze or glost firing. This is usually taken to a higher temperature than for the biscuit firing; earthenware being 1060°–1150°C. (cones 02–1) and stoneware 1250°–1280°C. (cones H8–H9). Glaze is made up of specially prepared glass-like mixture which melts in the kiln to form a smooth, even, waterproof covering. There are many different sorts of glaze: shiny and transparent, white, coloured, opaque, matt or textured.

Mixing up the glaze

Weigh the ingredients according to your recipe or stated instruction and add the powder to water. Leave it to stand and slake for an hour or so, then pass it through an 80-mesh sieve to ensure that it is smooth, even and free from lumps. Glaze thickness is difficult to judge at first, but generally it needs to be like single cream. Some glazes, however, need to be slightly thicker and some thinner.

Waxing

Pots fired to earthenware temperature are covered all over with glaze and stood on stilts in the kiln to prevent them sticking to the kiln shelf. Stoneware pots, however, must have glaze removed from the bottom as they must stand directly on the kiln shelf.

Likewise, where a lid sits in a pot the touching surfaces must be clean of glaze. This can most easily be done by painting on a wax emulsion solution before glazing. When dry, the wax resists the glaze; any drops which do stick can easily be wiped away with a sponge.

Dipping

Prepare the glaze, making sure it is the correct thickness. Applying glaze by dipping is the method which is quickest and gives the

Dipping glaze

most even results.

A glaze container is required, the inside of which is sufficiently large to completely immerse the pot. Make sure you have a large enough quantity of glaze.

Hold the pot as illustrated as this prevents air bubbles being trapped inside and

Dipping glaze outside

leaving bare, unglazed patches. Dip the pot in the glaze, gently twisting it round and leave it for 3–5 seconds. Turn the pot upside down to pour out the glaze and shake it gently to remove drops. Hold it until the glaze has lost its shine.

If you want to glaze only the outside hold the pot completely vertically and lower it into the glaze. Air trapped inside will prevent the glaze from entering.

Pouring

Large pots are more easily

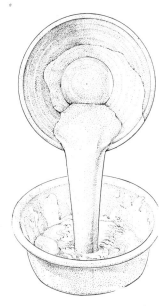

Preparing for the kiln

Let the pots dry before handling them and preparing them for the kiln. Wipe off any glaze from the bottom of the pots or from lid edges or galleys with a wet sponge. Clean off glaze 3 mm up the side. This ensures that the glaze will not run and stick to the kiln shelf.

Next, retouch the bare

glazed by pouring the glaze, first inside then out. Do the inside first by swilling round a good measure of glaze, and let this dry before doing the outside. This process should be done as quickly as possible so that an even covering is obtained. Where glaze overlaps, it will be thicker and look different. This feature can be incorporated as a decorative effect and used to give a more interesting inside surface.

The best method to use to glaze the outside of the pot depends on the size of the pot. It can either be held in the hand and tipped as the glaze is poured over so that the glaze covers it evenly, or can be supported on wooden strips across a bowl stood on a banding wheel. As the glaze is poured, the wheel can slowly be turned to enable a more even coating to be achieved.

patches. These will be where the pot has been held with the fingers or been supported on the rim. Blob rather than paint on the glaze as this helps it to build up the required thickness. Finally, rub down any large drips or thick runs of glaze with the fingers to get an even coating.

Once the pots are glazed, avoid handling them until they are packed into the kiln. This eliminates the chances of chipping the glaze.

Raw glazing

All these processes are described for use on biscuit fired pots, which are strong and can be handled safely. However, some pots can be glazed before they have been fired; this process is known as raw glazing because the pots are raw, or unfired. This certainly speeds up the process, as the biscuit firing is entirely omitted, but some clays will collapse if they have glaze added before they are fired. Nearly all clays can only be raw glazed one side at a time, first the inside, then the outside, allowing each to dry before further handling.

Raw glazes must be high in clay content (15–20%) to make it stick to the pot. It is a process worth trying on a none-too-treasured piece.

Decorating pots

Decoration can be either painted or sprayed onto the biscuit pot which is then covered with glaze. This is known as underglaze. Or it can be applied on top of the unfired glaze; this is known as in-glaze. Plain glazes usually show up the decoration more than textured coloured glazes. Traditionally, white opaque tin glazes have been used for majolica decoration, which is still a feature of much contemporary pottery made in Mediterranean countries.

Materials

Colours can be purchased as metal colouring oxides, of which the most popular are copper-green, cobalt-blue, iron-brown and manganese-mauve tan. All these can be mixed together to obtain various shades. Specially prepared pigments are known as underglaze colours and manufacturers offer a wide range of colours, most of which are intermixable.

Brushes are expensive and should be carefully washed after use. Japanese brushes with long bristles are excellent, as are specially made underglaze brushes.

Mixing colours

Metal oxides are more powerful weight for weight than underglaze colours and therefore less is needed. Mix the colours with a little water and a touch of glaze, using a palette knife to grind up the powder, on an old plate or sheet of glass.

Grind the powder as fine as you can; this prevents roughness and specking in the fired design.

Applying the design

Painting onto an absorbent surface like biscuit pottery or unfired glaze requires sure firm movements as each stroke tends to show in the fired designs. Outlines can be drawn first with a soft pencil, though this often spoils the freshness of the movements.

Designs painted under the glaze become softer than those painted on top. Colours can be sprayed using an artist's mouth atomiser. Designs can be developed using simple paper silhouettes. Lines can be banded on using the banding wheel.

▼ Decorated studio pottery. The red earthenware teapot has a wax resist decoration brushed onto the biscuit fired pot, which was then dipped in a white majolica tin glaze. Incised decoration with colour is used on the flat press-moulded earthenware dish shown at the back of the illustration. Thin washes of colour were used to give a pleasant, natural-looking effect.

On the bowl shown on the right, on-glaze painted decoration is used over a tin glaze and fired to around 1100°C. Vigorous brush strokes give this bowl great character. The faceted bowl was fired in a stoneware reduction kiln and has a bright coloured, orange glaze and wax resist decoration. The rich combination of brown inside the bowl and white outside, with orange decoration, is very successful.

Glaze firing

The second, or glaze, firing is slightly more complicated than the biscuit firing. The pots must be packed carefully so that they do not touch each other, yet kiln space must be used economically to enable as many pots to be included as possible. During the firing the glaze melts and spreads evenly over the surface of the pot. The firing temperature is critical. If it is too high the glaze will bubble and run; if it is too low the glaze will be rough and under-fired.

▲ Record the details of each firing in your log book. Show time, temperature and control setting. Also indicate the sort of wares in the kiln, whether they are large or small pieces.

Packing the kiln

First, sort out all the pots which are the same height as these can all be packed on the same shelf. Check each one to make sure there are no chipped rims or un-cleaned areas. Paint the inside of lids with a mixture of alumina 80 and china clay 20 to stop them sticking to the gallery.

Check the kiln shelves to see that they are clean and free of glaze. They can be cleaned by being rubbed with a carborundum stone. Paint a mixture of batt wash (alumina 80, china clay 20) on the shelves to stop the pots sticking.

Place the kiln props in position first, three to a shelf, and then put in the pots. In an earthenware firing carefully stand the pots on stilts.

The next shelf should stand a good 5 mm above the pots. Build up the shelf layers, placing the props directly over each other.

Finally place three cones in front of the spyhole: one at a lower temperature, one at the correct temperature and one at a higher temperature. When the middle cone bends the correct temperature has been reached and the kiln can be switched off.

▶ After the pots have been glaze-fired, rub the bottom of each pot with a carborundum stone. This is particularly important with earthenware pots as the stilts often leave sharp daggers of glaze which must be removed. Never rub your fingers over the base of the pot until it has been ground smooth.

Firing the kiln

Fire the kiln slowly for two hours, then close the vent at the top of the kiln; follow by two hours on medium setting, then full setting until top temperature is reached. Wait until the kiln has cooled to 100°C before opening the door and taking out the pots.

There is a great temptation to try to speed up the cooling and this must be avoided. Rapid cooling can result in cracking and can damage the kiln and cause the elements to collapse. The temptation to take a peep at the cooling pots should be resisted.

▼ A fired kiln cooling and waiting to be unpacked. This electric kiln takes 10–12 hours to fire to stoneware temperature and 24 hours to cool. The shelves are supported on wide props to spread the weights and prevent them from warping.

A home firing

Three simple methods are described here for potters to fire their own pots in a garden or yard The basic equipment required is kept to a minimum, the fuel (either wood or sawdust) being the most essential. These are essentially primitive kilns in that the pots are not kept separate from the flame. This means that the maximum temperature reached will be about 800°C and that no glaze can be used; instead the pots will be coloured and marked by the flame.

Points to watch

For any primitive firing, fire only small pots with fairly thin walls. Pots with thick walls are likely to break with the sudden rise in temperature. Before packing the pots, make quite sure they are bone dry. This can be done by placing them in a warm oven for an hour.

Make pots out of clay which contains good proportions of sand and grog as these act as openers which enable the clay to withstand the sudden temperature rise. It is the sudden temperature shock in the early part of firing which is the most critical breaking point.

The bonfire

Choose a day which is not too windy as this might cause the wood to burn too rapidly. In Nigeria, waiting for the right day is a necessary ingredient for success, though with the skills the potters have acquired the failure rate is very low.

Stand the warm pots on a bed of dry wood leaving gaps so that air can penetrate and allow the wood to burn.

Build up a good amount of dry wood around the pots so they are eventually covered with a pile of smallish wood. Put larger pieces over this, though take care that they will not fall and break the pots.

A bonfire firing

Bricks placed round the edge will contain the fire.

Burn the wood, adding more until a good sized pile of embers has formed by which time the pots will have been fired. Leave the embers to cool slowly; this can be delayed by laying sheets of corrugated metal or turfs of grass over the embers.

A pit firing

Pit firing

This method is one used by the Indians of North America. Dig a pit approximately 450 mm deep and stand the pots in it. The pit can be built out of bricks.

Place fire bars across the top and build a bonfire on this.

As the fire burns the hot ashes fall into the pit, slowly burying the pots. When the pots have been completely covered they will have been fired, though quite a lot of wood has to be burnt to get a pit full of embers.

Sawdust firing

This can be built inside any metal container from a square biscuit tin to a dustbin with air holes punched in the side. It can also be done by loosely building up bricks to form a round chamber.

Put a layer of sawdust at the bottom, stand pots on this and put another layer of sawdust on top. Repeat the process until the chamber is filled. Do not place the pots too close to one another, or they will not get hot enough. Start a small fire at the top to light the sawdust. This will gradually burn down, firing the pots as it does so.

A sawdust firing

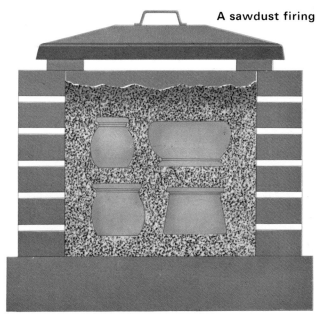

Craft societies

The Federation of British Craft Societies, 80A
Southampton Row, London WC1, 01-242 2209, exists to promote and protect the wellbeing of the craft movement, and to represent member societies and negotiate on their behalf.

The member societies, which are growing all the time, are usually local groups of craftsmen or groups of specialist craftsmen who have got together in an effort to assert their own status by arranging exhibitions and general activities for the general public. This process increases public awareness of the craft industry, maintains the high standards of craftsmanship and fosters interest in various crafts amongst laymen.

The level of activity in each society varies considerably. Some merely concentrate on organising an annual exhibition, others provide courses and lectures; at the very least they provide a means for the layman to contact local craftsmen in the subject of their interest.

The societies listed below, with the names of their Hon. Secs., have members who are potters. Suitably courteous approaches to them might well be rewarding for the enthusiastic amateur who may find a craftsman prepared to at least give a workshop tour. Any postal approach should naturally be attended by a stamped addressed envelope.

The Craftsmen's Circle of Pembrokeshire,
Mrs. A. Holden,
Four Bays,
Freshwater East,
Pembroke.

The Craftsmen Potters Association of Great Britain,
David Canter,
William Blake House,
Marshall Street,
London W.1.

Society of Craftsmen,
Mrs. C. Bulmer,
Old Kemble Galleries,
29 Church Street,
Hereford.

The Devon Guild of Craftsmen,
Mrs. Helen Hull,
3 Model Cottages,
Lower Town, Poundsgate,
Newton Abbot, Devon.

Ditchling Handworkers Guild,
Mrs. E. M. Warman,
Underhill Cottage,
Westmeston, Hassocks,
Sussex, BN6 8XG.

Guild of Gloucestershire Craftsmen,
George W. Brotherton,
Hambutts Barn,
Edge Lane,
Painswick,
Gloucestershire.

Red Rose Guild of Designer Craftsmen,
Anne-Marie Sillitoe,
29 Thick Hollins,
Meltham,
Huddersfield, H27 3DQ.

The Somerset Guild of Craftsmen,
Rev. R. D. F. Wild,
Railway House,
Stogumber,
Taunton,
Somerset, TA4 3TR.

South Wales Potters,
Grazia Gintz,
67 Pentwyn,
Radyr,
Cardiff,
South Glamorgan

Suffolk Craft Society,
Mrs. Rhonda Jacob,
33 Padley Water,
Chillesford,
Nr. Woodbridge,
Suffolk.

Surrey Crafts Association,
J. C. Hollinghurst,
c/o Bureau of Industrial Liaison,
University of Surrey,
Guildford,
Surrey.

Guild of Sussex Craftsmen,
Gordon Lawrie,
30 High Street,
Steyning,
Sussex, BN4 3GG.

The Cornwall Crafts Association,
Joan M. Lee,
The Chevin,
Seton,
Torpoint,
Cornwall.

West of England Association of Craftsmen,
Brillig Arts Centre,
8-9 New Bond Street,
Bath, Avon, BA1 1BE.

Guild of Yorkshire Craftsmen,
Mrs. Jean M. Roberts,
29 Warrier Avenue,
Pogmoor,
Barnsley,
Yorkshire.

The Bladon Society of Arts and Crafts,
Peter Strong,
The Bladon Gallery,
Hurstbourne Tarrant,
Andover,
Hampshire.

Society for Education through Art,
Mrs Sylvia Beaumont,
Bath Academy of Art,
Corsham,
Wiltshire, SN13 0DB

Norfolk Contemporary Crafts Committee,
Peter Lane,
The White House,
Keswick Road,
Cringleford,
Norwich, NR4 6UG.

Association of British Craftsmen,
G. D. Richardson,
57 Coombe Bridge Avenue,
Coombe Dingle,
Bristol, Avon, BF9 2LT

British Crafts Centre,
Michael Sellers,
43 Earlham Street,
London WC2.

Membership of the Federation of British Craft Societies is continually changing and it is therefore a good idea to consult them for an up-to-date list. There are of course other societies, and loose groups of craftsmen in other areas and contact may often be made by studying the local newspaper which may carry news items about arts and crafts activities, and watching out for notices in public libraries. Local institutes which offer part-time or evening courses also provide a good contact point as they employ specialist teachers who are often craftsmen themselves.

Courses

FULL-TIME VOCATIONAL COURSES
Degree courses in Ceramics, Production and Design (unless otherwise stated) are offered at the following colleges which should be approached direct for further information:

Bristol Polytechnic (3-D Design).
Brighton Polytechnic (Wood, metal, ceramics & plastics).
Corsham—Bath Academy of Art (3-D Design).
Farnham—West Surrey College.
Leicester Polytechnic (with glass design).

INNER LONDON
Camberwell School of Arts and Crafts.
Central School of Art and Design.
Goldsmith's College (post-graduate course).

GREATER LONDON
Chislehurst—Ravensbourne College of Art and Design (3-D Design).
Croyden College of Design & Technology (post-graduate course).
Middlesex Polytechnic (3-D Design).

Leicester Polytechnic (Ceramics, silver and glass).
Loughborough College of Art & Design.
Manchester Polytechnic.
Stoke-on-Trent—North Staffordshire Polytechnic (3-D Design, post-graduate course in industrial ceramic technology).

Stourbridge—Foley College of Further Education (3-D glass with ceramics).
Wolverhampton Polytechnic.
WALES
Cardiff College of Art (3-D Design).
SCOTLAND
Duncan of Jordanstone College of Art (pottery and ceramics).
Glasgow School of Art (also post-graduate).
NORTHERN IRELAND
Belfast—Ulster College, Northern Ireland Polytechnic (also some post-graduate).

Courses leading to a diploma qualification are offered at the following colleges:

Birmingham Polytechnic.
Bournemouth College of Art.
Braintree College of Further Education (studio pottery).
Brighton Polytechnic.
Chesterfield College of Art and Design (studio ceramics).
Derby College of Art and Technology.
Eastbourne College of Art & Design.
Lancaster & Morecambe College of Art and Crafts.

INNER LONDON
Barnet College of Further Education (foundation course).
Chelsea School of Art (studio pottery and ceramics).

GREATER LONDON
Croydon College of Design and Technology.
Epsom School of Art & Design.
Harrow College of Technology and Art (studio pottery).
Enfield—Middlesex Polytechnic (jewellery/ceramics).

Lowestoft School of Art.
Nuneaton—North Warwickshire College of Technology and Art.
Preston Polytechnic (industrial and studio ceramics).

Redruth—Cornwall Technical College.
Rochester—Medway College of Design (studio pottery).
Stafford College of Further Education (industrial ceramics).
Stoke-on-Trent—North Staffordshire Polytechnic.
Wallasey College of Further Education (industrial ceramics).
WALES
Carmarthen—Dyfed College of Art.
SCOTLAND
Dundee—Duncan of Jordanstone College of Art (pottery and ceramics).
Edinburgh College of Art.

If you are interested in any of these courses you should write direct to the colleges to obtain further information. Addresses can be obtained by consulting the Telephone Directories in your local reference library.

Application for degree courses is made to the **Universities Central Council on Admissions (UCCA),** PO Box 28, Cheltenham, Gloucestershire, GL50 1HY. Tel: Cheltenham (0242) 59091. Qualification for admission is usually based on a certain academic achievement by examination and in many cases on the successful completion of a "foundation year".

Many degree courses are registered with the **Society of Industrial Artists and Designers (SIAD)** and successful completion entitles the student to apply to the Society's Licentiatship (LSIA) though the award is not automatic.

The Certificate in Industrial Ceramics (CIC) is offered by some of the colleges listed in the diploma list above. This Certificate is offered in co-operation with the Stafford College of Art and Pottery Manufacturers. The course provides a comprehensive training for suitable students who wish to specialise in some branch of the pottery industry and to qualify as designer/craftsmen.

Further general information on vocational courses in ceramics can be obtained from:
Design Council, 28 Haymarket, London SW1Y 4SU. Tel: 01-839 8000.

FULL-TIME WORKSHOP TRAINING
Anyone who wishes to approach the subject from a more practical aspect could approach a professional potter direct with a view to becoming a trainee assistant. As no formal apprenticeship scheme exists the standard of teaching received in this way will depend on the enthusiasm of the potter concerned. Furthermore much of the potter's work is likely to be of a repititious nature and thus rather constricting to the trainee. Names and addresses of potters can be obtained from the bodies listed below. Any possible visits should be arranged beforehand.

Craftsmen Potters Association, William Blake House, Marshall Street, London W1.
Council of Small Industries in Rural Areas, 39 Camp Road, Wimbledon Common, London SW19.
Crafts Advisory Committee, 12 Waterloo Place, London SW1.

The Federation of British Craft Societies, 80A Southampton Row, London WC1 will provide a list of their member societies which if contacted will give information concerning potters operating in their areas.

When writing for information you should always enclose a stamp for reply.

PART-TIME COURSES
Most courses in this category do not fall into the classification "vocational". Some colleges offer their own certificate but by far the most popular courses are those classed as "recreational" which are generally "evening" classes.

These courses vary immensely not only in subject matter but also in the quality of teaching. Fees will usually be low, materials provided at a low cost and with reasonable instruction a year spent at a once-a-week evening class will give a good basic grounding in the techniques of pottery and ceramics.

Information about these courses can be obtained from your local education authority and in London from the publication *Floodlight* obtainable from newsagents. Even if no course is available in your area it is worth making an enquiry as often courses are provided on a supply and demand basis—your enquiry may thus tip the balance.

Short courses are sometimes offered by colleges or by individual potters. Such courses would usually happen in the summer and would tend to be expensive. However the level of tuition would tend to be high and good equipment is often available.

Details of these short courses can be obtained from a booklet "Residential Short Courses" published by **The National Institute of Adult Education** 35 Queen Anne Street, London W1M 0BL, also from the national press and such publications as *Ceramic Review,* 17A Newburgh Street, London W1, and *Pottery Quarterly,* Northfield Studio, Tring, Hertfordshire, and also from the Craftsmen Potters Shop (see above); and *Crafts* published by the **Crafts Advisory Committee,** 12 Waterloo Place, London SW1 4AV

Pottery on show

A large number of the museums and art galleries in the United Kingdom have good collections of ceramics from a variety of different periods. For a full list reference should be made to the annual publication "Museums & Galleries in Great Britain & Ireland"—an ABC Travel Guide published by ABC Travel Guides Ltd., Oldhill, London Road, Dunstable, Bedfordshire, LU6 3EB. This publication has a subject index which shows which particular museums have collections of ceramics.

The following list gives the location of museums with collections of particular interest and does not intend to be exhaustive. The starting point for investigation could well be your local museum or art gallery.

Alton: The Curtis Museum— English porcelain and studio pottery.
Barnard Castle (Co Durham): The Bowes Museum —late medieval to 19th century European.
Barnsley: Cannon Hall Museum and Art Gallery— 18th century.
Bath: The Holburne of Menstrie Museum of Art— 18th century. Victoria Art Gallery—Early ceramics.
Bedford: Cecil Higgins Art Gallery—Continental porcelain
Berwick-on-Tweed: Museum and Art Gallery— General ceramics.
Bideford: Museum—Devon pottery.
Bignor: Roman Villa Museum—Samian ware.
Birkenhead (Cheshire): Williamson Art Gallery and Museum—Della Robbia pottery and Liverpool porcelain.
Birmingham: City Museum and Art Gallery—General ceramics.
Bolton: Museum and Art Gallery—18th century English pottery.
Bootle (Lancashire): Museum and Art Gallery—Lancaster collection of English figured pottery, Bishop collection of Liverpool pottery.
Bournemouth: Rothesay Museum—English porcelain.
Brighton: Museum and Art Gallery—English slip ware.
Bristol: City Museum and Art Gallery—English and oriental ceramics.
Cambridge: Anthropological Museum—Prehistoric. Fitzwilliam Museum—General ceramics.
Carlisle: Museum and Art Gallery—Early regional examples.
Castleford: Area Library and Museum—Castleford pottery.
Ipswich: Christchurch

Mansion—18th century ceramics.
London: British Museum— All periods.
Fenton House—Binning collection of porcelain. Guildhall Museum—English medieval wares.
Horniman Museum— Ethnographical pottery. London Museum—Pottery connected with London's history.
Victoria & Albert Museum— General pottery and porcelain. Wallace Collection— Porcelain.
Manchester: Wythenshawe Hall—Royal Lancastrian Pottery.
Oxford: Ashmolean Museum —Early cultures.
Port Sunlight: Lady Lever Art Gallery—Wedgwood and Chinese ceramics.
Shrewsbury: Clive House— Shropshire ceramics.
Stoke-on-Trent: Hanley Museum—Staffordshire pottery and porcelain, also pottery from continent, orient, etc. Spode-Copeland Museum and Art Gallery—Early Spode Blue, Copeland and Garrett up to present.
Wedgwood Museum—Early Wedgwood ware (only by appointment)
Worcester: Dyson Perrins Museum—Old Worcester porcelain, finest collection of Worcester in the world.
Channel Islands
Guernsey—Hauteville House— General collection.
Northern Ireland
Belfast—Ulster Museum— Irish pottery.
SCOTLAND
Edinburgh: Lauriston Castle —General ceramics.
Glasgow: Burrell Collection— General porcelain.
WALES
Brecon: Brecknock Museum —Local pottery.

Book list

A Potters Book, B. Leach, Faber, 1945, £3.50.
For many potters this is the bible—practical advice and a philosophy very relevant to our lives today.

The Unknown Craftsman, S. Yanagi (adpt. B. Leach), Kodansha International, 1973, £8.40.
A well illustrated discussion of some of the best crafts made and a plea for higher standards and more humility in the artist.

Pottery in Britain Today, M. Casson, Tiranti, 1967, £5.00.
An illustrated survey of British pottery ten years ago.

Artist Potters in Britain, M. Rose, Faber, 1970, £6.50.
A well illustrated scholarly selective survey of some contemporary potters.

**Practical Pottery &
Ceramics,** K. Clark, Studio Vista, 1972, £1.25.
A beginner's guide covering all processes from making to selling.

**Illustrated Dictionary of
Practical Pottery,** R. Fournier, Van Nostrand Reinhold, 1969, £4.50.
Comprehensive technical, practical and historical information covering all the potter's needs, by a well established potter.

A History of Pottery, E. Cooper, Longman, 1972, £4.50.
A readable and comprehensively illustrated guide for the potter and layman written by a potter.

Stoneware & Porcelain, D. Rhodes, Pitman, 1960, £6.00.
An in-depth guide to the making and firing of high temperature wares.

**Kilns, Design, Construction
& Operation,** D. Rhodes, Pitman, 1969, £6.00.
An historical and practical account of the building and firing of all sorts of kilns, particularly recommended.

Technique of Pottery, D. Billington, Batsford, 1975, £3.95.
All pottery processes are included, written by a dedicated crafts-person.

English Slipware Dishes, R. Cooper, Tiranti, £5.00.
A beautifully illustrated and descriptive account of a very English group of wares.

**Kilns & Kiln Firing for the
Craft Potter,** H. Fraser, Pitman, 1969, £1.75.
A wordy guide on how to operate and fire commercial electric kilns.

**Tin Glazed Pottery in
Europe & The Islamic
World,** A. Caiger-Smith, Faber, 1973, £15.00.
A scholarly survey of some of the most richly decorated wares ever made.

Ceramics, P. Rawson, Oxford University Press, 1971, £2.50.
A general historical account of the whole area of ceramics.

Stoneware Glazes, C. Beck, Isles House, 1973, £1.85.
Recipes for slips and glazes for use at high temperatures.

The Technique of Throwing, J. Colbeck, Batsford, 1969, £4.50.
Photographic illustrations of many basic and advanced processes, especially useful for the home potter.

**Clay & Glazes for the
Potter,** D. Rhodes, Pitman, 1973, £6.00.
Most potters find this an indispensable guide to the behaviour of materials.

Simple Pottery, K. Drake, Studio Vista, 75p.
An inexpensive guide on how to make pottery without a wheel.

Pioneer Pottery, M. Cardew, Longmans, 1971, £4.50.
A wealth of advice and practical information. Aimed at the more advanced student.

Pottery, D. Winkley, Pelham Books, 1974, £4.00.
A guide to making pottery, running a workshop and kiln building: a craft potter's point of view.

New Ceramics, E. Lewenstein & E. Cooper, Studio Vista, £6.95.
A world-wide survey of contemporary work in all major countries (with the exception of China). Fascinating browsing.

Suppliers

The general suppliers listed below will send illustrated catalogues free of charge, which not only list materials and equipment but also contain much valuable information, particularly recommended are The Fulham Pottery, and Harrison-Mayer Ltd.

General suppliers

The Fulham Pottery Ltd.,
210 New Kings Road,
London SW6
Tel: 01-736 1188

Wengers Ltd.,
Etruria,
Stoke-on-Trent,
Staffordshire ST4 7BQ
Tel: 0782-25126

Podmore and Sons Ltd.,
Shelton,
Stoke-on-Trent,
Staffordshire.
Tel: 0782-24571

Harrison-Mayer Ltd.,
Meir,
Stoke-on-Trent,
Staffordshire ST3 7PX
Tel: 0782-316111

R. J. W. Ratcliffe & Sons Ltd.,
Rope Street,
off Shelton New Road,
Stoke-on-Trent,
Staffordshire ST4 6DJ
Tel: 0782-611321

Ferro Ltd.,
Wombourne,
Wolverhampton WV5 8DA
Tel: 090-77 4144

Kiln suppliers

Cromartie Kilns Ltd.,
Park Hall Road,
Longton,
Stoke-on-Trent,
Staffordshire
Tel: 0782-313947

Kilns and Furnaces Ltd.,
Keele Street Works,
Tunstall,
Stoke-on-Trent,
Staffordshire
Tel: 0782-84642

Catterson-Smith Ltd.,
Adams Bridge Works,
South Way,
Exhibition Grounds,
Wembley,
Middlesex HA9 0HN
Tel: 01-902 4291

Laboratory and Research Furnace Co. Ltd.,
Railway Street,
Bridgeworth,
Shropshire
Tel: 095-245 3158

Kasenit Ltd.,
Denbigh Road,
Bletchley,
Buckinghamshire
Tel: 0908 79474

Kiln furniture suppliers

Acme Marls Ltd.,
Clough Street,
Hanley,
Stoke-on-Trent,
Staffordshire
Tel: 0782-21541

Clay suppliers

Potclays Ltd.,
Brickkiln Lane,
Etruria,
Stoke-on-Trent,
Staffordshire
Tel: 0782-29816

Watts, Blake, Bearne, & Co. Ltd.,
Park House,
Courtney Park,
Newton Abbot,
Devon
Tel: 0626 2345

Moira Pottery Co. Ltd.,
Moira,
Near Burton-on-Trent,
Staffordshire
Tel: 0283-221961

English China Clay Co,
John Keay House,
St Austell,
Cornwall
Tel: 0726 4482

Brushes and special tools

Alec Tiranti,
72 Charlotte Street,
London W1
Tel: 01-636 8565

Wheels

Judson and Hudson Ltd.,
Parker Street Works,
Keighley,
Yorkshire
Tel: 05352-2016

Woodley's Potters Wheels Ltd.
Newton Poppleford,
Devon
Tel: 03956-666

Wengers Ltd.,
Etruria,
Stoke-on-Trent,
Staffordshire ST4 7BQ
Tel: 0782 25126

Pilling Pottery,
Pilling,
Preston,
Lancashire.
Tel: 039-130 307

Glossary

Absorption: the soaking up of water by either a fired or unfired clay body.

Agate ware: made in imitation of mixed natural stones such as agate by using different coloured clays.

Ball clay: highly plastic, fine-grained sedimentary clay often added to less plastic clays.

Banding wheel—"whirler": a metal wheel-head revolved by hand used when decorating a pot or simply for turning the pot without damage.

Batt: a flat portable working surface useful for making or storing pots.

Battwash: mixture of flint, alumina, china clay, and water painted on kiln shelves to prevent pots sticking to the shelves or old glaze spots.

Biscuit: pottery which has been fired to an insoluble but porous state, like a plant pot.

Body: the clay which forms the structure or fabric of a pot.

Calcine: to heat a ceramic material to a moderate temperature to drive off chemical water and carbon dioxide.

China clay—kaolin: a pure clay which fires almost white, one of the components of porcelain.

Coiled pottery: hand-made pottery in which rolls of clay are built one upon the other in rings, or in a continuous spiral, to make a hollow shape.

Composite pots: ware which is the result of assembling separate units, possibly made by different techniques. Thus a composite candelabra may have a slab plinth, a coiled stem and thrown candle-holders.

Crazing: the cracking of the glaze on the surface of pottery caused by greater contraction in the glaze than in the pot during cooling. Called crackle when used decoratively.

Deflocculant: a substance which, acting chemically on plastic clay, gives it liquid characteristics with the addition of very little water, e.g. sodium silicate and sodium carbonate.

Delftware: Tin-glazed earthenware named after the Dutch town of Delft.

Earthenware: glazed pottery fired to a temperature of about 1000–1100°C and in which the body becomes only slightly vitrified, usually red or brown with a comparatively open-grained structure and low chipping resistance.

Flux: a melting agent which causes silica to form glaze or glass, such as frit, feldspar, lime, lead or borax.

Frit: a compounded glass which has been fired and fused, used to render glaze materials insoluble and to make lead non-toxic.

Glaze: thin coating of special sort of glass applied to the surface of the clay, used as decoration and to render it waterproof.

Glost: glaze or glazed, thus a glost firing is the firing of glazed ware.

Green: unfired pots are described as "green" or "green ware" when they are dry and awaiting their first firing.

Grog: crushed or ground hard-fired clay added to plastic clay to quicken drying, to add texture or decrease shrinkage.

Kidney: a kidney-shaped tool made of flexible steel for finishing pots thrown on the wheel, or made of stiff rubber for pressing and smoothing clay in a mould.

Kiln: a refractory clay lined furnace for firing ceramic ware.

Kneading: working the clay with the hand to obtain an even texture throughout, and expel air bubbles.

Lawn: a sieve with fine mesh made from phosphor bronze.

Leatherhard—Cheesehard: condition of clay when it is too firm to bend yet soft enough to be carved.

Matt glaze: a dull-surfaced glaze, lustreless and non-reflecting.

Maturing temperature: the temperature at which a glaze exhibits its best qualities; a variation of 10°C on either side can be enough to spoil the result.

On-glaze: enamel decoration on ware which has been already glazed and fired.

Oxidation: complete combustion when firing takes place with an adequate supply of oxygen, as in electric kilns.

Pinch pot: simple hand-made pot made by "pinching" into shape a ball of clay.

Plasticity: the property of clay which allows it to be worked and reshaped without cracking.

Porcelain: white form of stoneware usually translucent, made from clay prepared from feldspar, china clay, and flint. Hard and non-porous, the most highly refined of all clay bodies and requiring the highest firing.

Porous: describes material which allows water to seep through, i.e. a plant pot.

Pyrometer: an instrument for registering the exact temperature of the kiln.

Pyrometric cones: slender pyramids of ceramic material made in a graded series which at certain temperatures soften and bend indicating that the clay and glazes which take a certain time and temperature to mature have done so.

Raw clay: unfired clay.

Raw glazing: applying glaze to an unfired pot, and heating both clay and glaze together, to produce what is known as once-fired ware.

Reduced: fired in oxygen-starved atmosphere, usually used with stoneware to affect the colour of metal oxides in the glaze.

Refractory: material with a high temperature resistance.

Rib: a tool used in throwing to smooth and form the surfaces of the pots.

Saggar: a protective refractory box to hold pottery in fuel-burning kilns to protect the pots from the flames.

Saltglaze: produced by tossing salt into a hot stoneware kiln: the salt vapourizes and combines with the surface of the clay to form a glaze.

Slab pottery: hand-built pottery made by assembling flat slabs of clay.

Slip: clay in a very liquid, smooth state, which can be used for trailed or marbled decoration.

Slip-casting: an industrial technique in which slip is poured into plaster of Paris moulds to form pots.

Slip trailing: decorative process involving leaving trails of slip over the surface of the ware.

Slipware: pottery, normally lead-glazed, decorated with white or coloured slips.

Slurry: clay mixed with water, used as potter's "glue"

Stoneware: glazed pottery in which both body and glaze are fused together in a non-porous vitrified state, as a result of firing to temperatures usually above 1200°C.

Throwing: the technique of making pots with the hands from plastic clay on a wheel.

Tin glaze: earthenware glaze made opaque by the addition of tin ashes.

Turning: the technique of trimming thrown pots using metal and other tools when the pots have become leather-hard.

Viscous: stiff and unmoving. Glaze is usually viscous, which makes it stay on the pot during the firing when the glaze has melted.

Vitreous: glass-like. Usually refers to a stoneware or porcelain fired body.

Warping: distortion in a pot caused by non-uniform drying or uneven ware thickness, or from being fired in a kiln which does not heat evenly.

Wedging: the cutting and re-forming of lumps of plastic clay preparatory to kneading to ensure an even texture.

Wheel-head: the circular flat disc attached to the revolving spindle of a potter's wheel, and on which the pot is formed.

Index

Credits

Contributing potters

The publishers would like to thank the Craftsmen Potters Association for the loan of work by the following potters for use in the photographs:

Page 7: Deidre Burnett, David Leach, Peter Stoodley.
Page 44: Joan Hepworth, Hoon Ai Ooi, Colin Kellam, Alan Wallwork.
Page 49: Ladi Kwali.
Page 81: Aldermaston Pottery, Andrew Holden, John Maltby.

Artists

Mike Gorman

Ilric Shetland
QED

Photographs

Art and Antiques Weekly: contents, 17, 23, 59
Benteli Verlag, Bern: 24
British Ceramic Research Association: 15
British Museum: 11 (top), 16
Peter Clayton: 4
Peter Dick: 5, 13
Fitzwilliam Museum, Cambridge: 26
Paul Forrester: 7, 44, 49, 51, 53, 55, 56, 73, 77, 81
John Freeman: 18
Michael Holford: 17, 27
Peter Kinnear: 31
Kunsthistorische- Museum. Vienna: 22
London Borough of Ealing: 31
Mary Evans Picture Library: 26
McQuitty International Collection: 10
J. Mellaart: 6
Britt- Ingrid Persson: 32
Dudley Reed: 36- 7, 38- 9, 41 43, 46- 7, 48- 9, 59, 60- 73, 83
Rien Bazen: 33
Royal Copenhagen Porcelain Co. Ltd.: 30
Sotheby, Parke, Bernet & Co.: contents
Tokyo Art Gallery: 21
Victoria and Albert Museum Crown copyright: 11 (below), 18, 20, 28
Josiah Wedgwood & Sons Ltd.: contents, 30
Zefa (UK): contents

Cover

Design: Design Machine
Photograph: Paul Forrester